Love, Gravity,
And God

Love, Gravity, And God:

Paul Tillich and the Existential
Depths of Reason and Religion

JEREMY D. YUNT

Barred Owl Books
Santa Barbara, CA

Love, Gravity, and God: Paul Tillich and the Existential Depths of Reason and Religion

Copyright © 2015 by Jeremy D. Yunt. All rights reserved. No portion of this book, except for brief review, may be reproduced, stored in a retrieval system, or transmitted in any form or by any means—electronic, mechanical, photocopying, recording, or otherwise—without written permission of the author.

Foreword
by Dr. Paul Lee

ISBN: 9798635717950

I dedicate this book to my mother and father

TABLE OF CONTENTS

Foreword ix
Introduction xiii

1 Fundamentalism and the Loss of Depth in Religion 1
2 Re-imagining Faith and God 21
3 Reason as Essential to Religion 47
4 Miracles, Revelation, and the Experience of Ecstasy 63
5 Existentialism, the Spiritual Presence,
   and the Conquest of Religion 73
6 Sin and Evil 99
7 Science, Spirit, and the "Multidimensional
   Unity of Life": The Case Against Supernaturalism 107
8 Jesus as "the Christ," "New Being," and
   "Final Revelation" 117
9 Salvation as Healing 135
10 The Eternal, and Ideas on What
    Happens After Death 147

Endnotes 159
About the Author 169

FOREWORD
by Dr. Paul Lee

When I was a student at St. Olaf College in Minnesota, Paul Tillich came to lecture on existentialism. I didn't understand a word he said. Neither did my roommates. They thought it was his fault, and I knew it was ours. His thick German accent certainly didn't help things. Nonetheless, that day something in Tillich's voice and demeanor resonated in me. I had found my teacher. Soon after, I followed Tillich to Harvard to do my doctoral work, eventually becoming his teaching assistant for the last two years of his esteemed professorship there.

When I got married I was eager to introduce my new bride to Tillich, who was as eager to meet her. But when they met, instead of saying "hello," she exclaimed, "I'm an atheist!" Tillich threw up his arms and said: "Wonderful! It means you are still searching!" This kind of playful openness exemplified Tillich's natural ability to connect with someone, even in a seemingly adversarial situation, albeit a harmless one here.

On top of this, for myself and the vast majority of his listeners—particularly the throng of students who flocked to his classes—Tillich was the great formulator. Regardless of what he was assessing—modern art, psychoanalysis, philosophy, science and technology, politics, history, culture—he knew how to "put it." He's one of the few academics I've encountered in my life who had a seeming encyclopedic knowledge of the world, a deep read into the existential concerns of humanity, and an ability to make you feel like his words were speaking directly to *you*. Watching him at work was an astounding thing to observe.

That first lecture at St. Olaf brought out one of Tillich's most prescient and ominous insights, one which still haunts me to this day: "We are living in the late stage of the self-destruction of industrial society, as a world above the given world of nature." This oft-repeated phrase of his became a sort of mantra to me over my years of teaching, research, and writing. The existentialist movement Tillich often spoke of—which he saw as a protest against the pernicious objectification of humans and nature under industrialization—analyzed the growing spiritual malaise and sense of meaninglessness so evident in modern society.

Uncharacteristic for a theologian of his time, Tillich believed that having empathy for nature and its nonhuman beings was crucial to our experience of life's depth. It's my contention, as well as Yunt's, that Tillich was perhaps the first "ecotheologian." He was writing about the profanization of nature decades before the term "ecological crisis" was even coined, and long before the publication of Rachel Carson's *Silent Spring* in 1962, which is largely viewed as the year of a nascent ecological consciousness. Tillich saw existentialism as partly rooted in the fight against the alienating effects and forced adjustment to a synthetic, hyper-rationalized existence we were creating faster than we could understand or cope with—a human creation detrimental to all realms of existence.

The rapid increase in neuroses and mental disease associated with modern human "progress" betrays this, and it's why he saw technology as a glaring symbol of our predicament. Its effects on humanity are seen today in the obsession with all things "virtual," "simulated," and "artificial"—all of which require the efficient commodification of nature, and even humans. The word "ecosystem" has even been co-opted by the regnant business class of late-stage capitalism. A collective escape from the real seems to be our modern hallmark, and we are only beginning to experience the fallout from this allegiance.

In the end, industrial society has sold us a bill of goods for which there seems no redemption. Tillich understood and analyzed the implications of this state of affairs better than anyone, always articulating the cultural, scientific, philosophical, and especially religious significance of humanity's evolving self-interpretation. An example of this came in one of my proudest moments, as I accompanied Tillich to one of his major addresses at M.I.T. in the 1960s on how science has changed humanity's view of itself. It was a missive aimed at the servants of industrial society, where the students referred to themselves as "tools," with a note of resignation and sarcasm. It was a profound experience to witness, and the irony was not lost on either of us.

In my own research, I have focused much on Tillich's existential philosophical masterpiece *The Courage to Be*, and it has become my favorite work of his. As a result, *thymos*—the Greek word for "courage" and the central theme of the book—is a pivotal word for me. It is Tillich's effort to restore the middle realm between reason and desire, i.e., the realm of human vitality. This is the deep self-affirmation of life in the face of its challenges and ambiguities, an overcoming of the subject-object split in our search for knowledge, and the establishment of a bodily basis for spirituality.

In *Love, Gravity, and God*, Yunt shares his high estimation of Tillich as a seminal thinker, analyzer of modern science and culture, and philosophical interpreter of religion. He unveils for us Tillich's quest for honest, meaningful answers to the questions, doubts, and perplexities brought about by distorted ideologies, e.g., scientific materialism and fundamentalist Christian theology. Regarding the latter, Tillich did not accept easy, static, or simple answers, and for this reason he was often at odds theologically and philosophically with the simple messages he heard mainstream fundamentalist evangelists filling the airwaves and television stations with. Instead, Tillich offered meaningful answers to life's difficult questions and challenges, even if he knew these answers weren't final or written in stone.

Yunt provides us with an outstanding introduction to Tillich's thought, laying out his key concepts in understandable terms. This book is an expression of Yunt's own vitality and "courage to be," and a superb exposition of Tillich's constant striving for truth through reason—with the goal of better understanding matters of Ultimate Concern.

Santa Cruz, CA

INTRODUCTION

Aside from growing fundamentalist extremism in the world's primary religions, as well as a rise in modern quasi-religions such as Scientology and Mormonism, mainstream religion is on the ropes. Church membership in Protestantism and Catholicism, the two main branches of Christianity, is in decline year after year. Reasonable people are increasingly looking for answers to their problems and concerns in other realms of life: friends, family, philosophy, science, psychology, New Age teachings, technology, yoga, science fiction, drugs, alcohol— anywhere other than old-time religion. And some of these are valid, incredibly helpful places to seek guidance. Some, of course, are not. But we have to wonder why mainstream religion is in such decline, and why the word "religion"—as opposed to "spiritual"— is itself in such disrepute in the modern world.[1] I believe there are several reasons.

The first is that a large number of people professing Christianity today are serving up nonsensical and/or supernatural ideas that just don't square with the way common sense, rationally-minded people see and understand reality. These peddlers of modern Christianity fail to understand that many biblical stories are symbolic, mythical pieces of literature not meant as literal reports of events. Unfortunately, this literal understanding of the Bible is the most simplistic and easy way to read and teach it, and most people want very simple ideas to accept and believe, even if these ideas are extreme or fly in the face of modern scientific discoveries— such as the belief that the earth is only 6,000 years old.

Second, though it's nothing new to religion in general, Christianity is today riddled with a staggering degree of hypocrisy. In Catholicism we have rampant, systemic child sexual abuse, a rigid and hierarchical power structure claiming the divine ability to impart salvation to its followers, and a blatant materialistic hoarding in the face of desperate poverty around the globe. Regarding the latter, I speak of the vast Vatican wealth that does not filter down to its millions of impoverished believers—the "least of these," of which Jesus said we should be most concerned. Granted, Catholicism does finally have a Pope (Francis) who clearly understands the essentially anti-materialistic message of Jesus, but the privileged, elitist hierarchical structure still remains.

Meanwhile, in modern evangelical Protestantism we have a long list of moral, legal, and economic transgressions perpetrated by popular church leaders—some leading to actual jail time. Added to all this is the strange theological perversion we see in a new breed of televangelists who preach the rather stupefying "gospel of prosperity"[2]—a belief system so at odds with the explicit anti-materialism of Jesus that we have to wonder how these people can call themselves "Christian."

On top of all this, religion is showing just how violent its ideologies can become. I speak mostly of the rise of modern Islamic terrorism, although we certainly can't forget the incredibly violent Catholic Inquisition that led to the death of thousands of innocent people throughout Europe. The centuries between then and now show that violence is nothing new to distorted religious ideology. And it calls into question how, in our so-called advanced, modern era religion can still be used to cause so much harm.

I wrote this book to shed light on a number of troublesome ideas religion engenders today—ideas threatening its credibility, relevance, and moral authority. And to do this with the greatest effect, I rely on the man widely considered the most significant Western religious thinker of the past century, Dr. Paul Tillich (1886-1965). The book you hold is my simplified interpretation and synopsis of one of the most profound religious texts ever written: Tillich's 900-plus page, three-volume *Systematic Theology*.[3] For those who've never heard Tillich's name before, he's the Protestant theologian and philosopher who reinterpreted and revolutionized Christianity for the modern world. I'm not talking about the popularized, watered-down Christianity you see peddled on television. Rather, I'm talking about the historically analyzed, philosophically sophisticated, and spiritually deep version of religion that comes from critical academic study and immersion.

There are a few historical precedents regarding Tillich that are worth noting here. Though he died back in 1965, his legacy is enduring and significant enough that even today we see his ideas being passed off by such famous New Age teachers as Eckhart Tolle—though, regrettably, Tolle never acknowledges his obvious indebtedness to Tillich. And prior to this, in the early 1950s, Martin Luther King, Jr. wrote his doctoral dissertation on Tillich's conception of God. But perhaps most significant, at the outset of World War II, Tillich was the first non-Jewish German intellectual Hitler expelled from his teaching position—as head of the philosophy department at the University of Frankfurt.

With penetrating scholarship, in his 1933 publication *The Socialist Decision*, Tillich rebuked the Fuhrer's ideology as a "bad form of political romanticism," leading to large public burnings of the book by the Nazis. In spite of the danger posed to him personally, Tillich was one of few academics with the courage to physically defend Jewish students on campus when they were attacked by Nazi "brown shirts." This experience is in sharp contrast to that of fellow philosopher Martin Heidegger, who Tillich taught with at the University of Marburg from 1924-1925. Though Heidegger significantly influenced Tillich's thought, rather than decrying the dangers of National Socialism like Tillich, Heidegger embraced it for some time—a decision he eventually came to regret.

In 1933, around the time of his publication of *The Socialist Decision*, Tillich was also being followed by the Gestapo. This, along with his dismissal from his teaching post, led to a hasty exile from his German homeland. Luckily, at the age of 47, and with virtually no experience with the English language, he was able to make it to America with a teaching offer from New York's Union Theological Seminary. The offer came from another great American theologian, Reinhold Niebuhr, who was deeply impressed with Tillich's theological, philosophical, and political writings. Astoundingly, Tillich mastered the English language in a very short time and vowed never to publish in German again. Considering the complexity of his ideas and the language it requires to explain them, this was no small feat.

His teaching career took him from Union Theological Seminary, to Columbia University (where he taught philosophy), to Harvard, and finally to the University of Chicago. At Harvard, Tillich was one of only five "University Professors"—the highest ranking one could attain at the institution. This allowed him to lecture in any department at the university. Toward the end of his life, he also taught for several semesters at the University of California at Santa Barbara, where he was offered a full professorship in 1965. However, at this same time he was also offered a professorship at the acclaimed New School for Social Research in New York City, which he accepted. Unfortunately, Tillich died of a heart attack on October 22nd, 1965.

Tillich was described by his former Harvard teaching assistant, Dr. Paul Lee, as a "one-man theological orchestra." I couldn't agree more. Tillich has an astounding, unique, and incredibly reasonable understanding of the complex topic of religion. Though he had a vast understanding of most of the world's religions, he was ultimately a Christian theologian—a Christian "existentialist" theologian, to be exact. This existentialist bent to his thought is what allowed him to absorb, analyze, and critique almost all realms of human thought and action. It's also what led him into a series of personal encounters and academic dialogues with seminal Buddhist teachers, most notably Zen master and professor of philosophy, Shin'ichi Hisamatsu. From this, Tillich developed a very deep interest in, and understanding of, Buddhism. Toward the end of his life he even lamented that he wished he could go back and rewrite his *Systematic Theology* after these encounters.

My intention with this book is simple. I will present, in as clear language as possible, the basic ideas of Tillich. Specifically, I will highlight the most essential philosophical, theological, psychological, cultural, and even scientific/ecological ideas found in the three volumes of his *Systematic Theology*. While I mainly want to translate his complex ideas into simple, clear language the average person can understand, I think it's also important to let Tillich's own words speak to you; this is why I often quote him at length. If you have a good understanding of philosophy and/or theology, this will be of immense benefit to you. However, if you don't have this background, I will follow the more challenging quotes with a summation of what his words mean in layperson's terms. I will also take the liberty of adding a few of my own thoughts relating his ideas to the world we live in today. Of necessity, some of his ideas will be left out, and perhaps not everyone familiar with his thought will agree exactly with my presentation of them; this is always the risk in interpreting someone else's thought.

I must also point out that, because of the time in which he was writing, the word "man" was always used when speaking of humanity as a whole. If Tillich were writing today he would, of course, use more inclusive, gender-neutral language. If at all possible, don't let this past mode of writing tarnish or overshadow your reading of the actual ideas Tillich is expressing. With that disclaimer, let's now get to the heart of this human endeavor we call "religion."

Three Basic Religious Questions... and Problems in Modern Religion Keeping Us from Answering Them

If ever there was a time we could use some reason when it comes to the topic of religion, it surely is now. Why? Because a person's religious views have profound effects on other people's lives, as well as on the planet itself (see my other related publication regarding this topic: *Faithful to Nature: Paul Tillich and the Spiritual Roots of Environmental Ethics*). In our technological age, these effects are of no small consequence. In fact, the negative effects of unreasonable religious ideology, coupled with our advanced technological power, form the basis of our world's deep existential threats. If we are to escape this threat, then reason must prevail—especially in the realm of morality and religion.

When talking about religion and reason—which, unfortunately, most people think mix like water and oil—it's important to remember that the essence of religion is really quite simple. It basically seeks to answer some fundamental human questions: *Why am I here on earth?; how can I live my life in the most meaningful way?; and what does life ultimately mean?* I believe the second question is really the heart of the matter when it comes to religion, and I ask you to constantly keep these three questions in mind as you move forward in this book. In the end, if we can get some solid, reasonable answers to these questions then we're making some real progress. And with the help of Tillich, that's exactly what I aim to do.

The book you hold is founded on a simple belief: the modern, popular understanding of Christianity is based on several major distortions. Oddly enough, these distortions are not primarily put forth by the opponents of religion. Rather, they are professed by the very followers of Christianity. What are these distortions? The most basic one is that the cornerstone of religious belief is the acceptance of ideas and stories that cannot be proven; this belief in the unbelievable, or the supernatural, is termed "faith." Here, faith is equated with suspending our need to reason, in the hopes of some unknown thing being proven after we die. . . and being rewarded for holding this belief. If you're like most people, you've heard this concept of faith put forth by televangelists, pastors of mega-churches, in the popular media, in the scientific reactions against it, and perhaps even by your own pastor or priest.

The problem is that faith is something other than belief in the unbelievable or unknown; such belief should be called for what it is—belief in magic and the supernatural. But it should not be called "faith." Regardless of this distortion of the concept of faith, millions of Christians today seem just as enthusiastic as ever about their belief in the unbelievable. The problem is that enthusiasm without proper knowledge— which in religion can lead to fanaticism—can have concrete, detrimental effects on other people and the world. These effects can manifest within ourselves (psychological), in our relations with other humans (ethical-social), and in our relations with the very planet that sustains us (ecological). Simply put, beliefs ultimately translate into action. And if certain beliefs lead to harmful actions, then we need to examine and, if necessary, debunk such harmful beliefs.

Though one should not be compelled to hold onto ideas that run counter to scientific facts, we still have to accept that what religion points to is in many ways mystifying and often transcends our common idea of reason. We are sometimes shaken by experiences that confound our everyday understanding of ourselves, others, and the world. So while I want to shed the light of reason onto religion, Tillich will show us that the sometimes perplexing nature of human existence still causes many of us to use words like "paradox," "miracle," and "mystery." Tillich will, however, reinterpret these terms more accurately to express their originally intended meanings—meanings which still retain the validity and soundness of scientific reason.

In addition to understanding faith as belief in the unbelievable, most Christians are also usually a bit obsessed with who, what, or where they will be after they die. As such, they see this life largely as a dress rehearsal for the "real" life they will live beyond the grave. Their concept of "salvation" centers on a deliverance, or escape, from this world. And at the same time that some Christians subscribe to this escapist thinking, many also fall prey to the false religious doctrine that, while on earth, God wants us to be materially successful (the "gospel of prosperity" I mentioned earlier): If we are materially successful, then surely it's a sign God is pleased with us. The fact that a great number of the largest Christian churches today preach this theologically shallow gospel of monetary wealth—overlooking the exploitation and material hoarding at its root—is evidence of this problem. The New Testament message of social and economic justice, the very foundation of Jesus' message, is somehow shockingly ignored by these churches.

Many rational, caring people today also have a difficult time with the large number of theological statements that seem odd or un-understandable. These statements often bring up more questions and confusions than they do answers. One striking example is the statement "Jesus died for our sins." To many people, this begs a lot of questions. Why would an innocent man have to be murdered to bring about our salvation? And what if I'm someone who is born and dies without ever hearing about Jesus? Does that mean I have no chance of salvation? Or what about the statement concerning Jesus that, in him, "God became man." Because of this statement, many Christians believe that Jesus is, in fact, God. In the following pages we will find this not only logically impossible, but also unbiblical.

These are just a few examples of why religion seems either off-the-mark or just plain nonsensical to a lot of people today. They are also the reason Tillich states the following: "Unfortunately, there are always theologians who indulge in the production of propositions which have no meaning semantically and who, in the name of the Christian faith, insist that one has to accept them in order to be a true Christian. They argue that divine truth is above human reason."[4] As the title of my book suggests, we'll find that basic human reason—rather than being below a divine reason, or somehow not useful in the realm of religion—is actually one of our main avenues into a better understanding of the true essence of religion.

As Tillich sees it, if one fails to use one's reason to understand the nuances of religious concepts, then it's quite easy to fall prey to what he calls a "sentimentalized religion." What he means by this is essentially a simplistic version of religion that, in the end, leads to its distortion—perhaps even its ultimate demise. And religious distortions are exactly what drove Tillich to express himself in the way he did. He saw an impoverishment of thought in most modern interpretations of religion, both on the side of those defending Christianity *and* on the side of those criticizing it. Therefore, his task was double-edged: first, to undercut the narrow and distorted explanations of religion offered by popularized Christianity (particularly fundamentalism), while second, providing a solid, reasoned defense of the Christian message to the more educated segments of society—the skeptics, scientists, philosophers, "atheists," artists, and anyone else who might have been turned away from religion by its supernatural and simplistic distortions.

This second part of his task is why Tillich was hailed during his life as an "apostle to the intellectuals." And he summed up his mission as an inside critic by saying: "It is a general characteristic of prophetic criticism of a religious tradition that it does not come from outside but from the center of the tradition itself, fighting its distortions in the name of its true meaning."[5] This led Tillich to speak of the various "demonizations" of Christianity throughout history: the persecution of "heretics," the wars against various Christian sects during the Inquisition, the supposed infallibility of the pope, and the fanatical anti-science and anti-intellectualism of modern fundamentalism.[6] To Tillich, all of these exposed the hypocrisy and intolerance he saw bringing Christianity closer and closer to its own undoing.

This, of course, makes us ask some obvious questions: How has religion, which in its essence is supposed to be a force for good in the world, ended up causing so many problems throughout history? With all the knowledge we've gained throughout the centuries, why do we still fight each other over religion? Why have the world's scientific and technical advancements not led to a more humane world? And what part has religion played in all this? Without further ado, let's let Tillich answer these and many, many other pertinent questions.

1

FUNDAMENTALISM AND THE LOSS OF DEPTH IN RELIGION

Tillich wasted no time in confronting what he saw as the primary problem in modern Christianity: fundamentalism. In the very first paragraph of the introduction to his *Systematic Theology*, he says:

> Fundamentalism fails to make contact with the present situation, not because it speaks from beyond every situation, but because it speaks from a situation of the past. It elevates something finite and transitory to infinite and eternal validity. In this respect fundamentalism has demonic traits. It destroys the humble honesty of the search for truth, it splits the conscience of its thoughtful adherents, and it makes them fanatical because they are forced

> to suppress elements of truth of which they are dimly aware.[7]

The essence of Christian fundamentalism is that literally everything in the Bible comes from a supernatural source and, therefore, is absolutely true and accurate. It treats religion as a set of divine truths that came from a heavenly realm centuries ago; it is up to us to simply accept everything in the Bible without question. To Tillich, this is a complete misunderstanding of religion. The problem with fundamentalism is that it fails to account for numerous facts conflicting with its literal interpretation of the Bible. It does this by ignoring or downplaying the historical, philosophical, cultural, political, psychological, scientific, and economic factors shaping the events in the Bible. And when it ignores these things it distorts the essence of religion.

One significant example of this is seen in the fundamentalist adherence to belief in supernatural events, such as the stories of Adam, Eve, and the serpent; Noah and the ark; and the creation of the universe in six days—to name just a few. When fundamentalism defends these events as literal historical occurrences, it splits the universe into a natural and a supernatural realm. In doing this, it places more value and emphasis on supernatural things, which in turn lessens the importance of life on earth—even causing humans to ignore or deny basic scientific facts.

In placing such emphasis on the supernatural, fundamentalism also requires us to accept a three-leveled understanding of existence: a heaven (supernatural), an earth (natural), and an underworld, or hell (supernatural). Firmly against this multi-leveled, anti-scientific understanding of reality, Tillich offers us his alternate vision: "In a vision of the universe which has no basis for a tripartite view of cosmic space in terms of earth, heaven, and underworld (hell), theology must emphasize the symbolic character of spatial symbols, in spite of their rather literal use in Bible and cult."[8] In other words, the symbols of heaven and hell should be seen for what they are—symbols, and not physical locations in the universe. In a later chapter, we'll examine Tillich's theory of the "multidimensionality unity of life," where we'll see a vision of reality in which all elements of existence are intimately enmeshed in every other one, and where there can be no absolute division between realms of total goodness and total evil, or natural and supernatural.

In essence, fundamentalism falters by requiring the acceptance of doctrines we cannot know or prove. This belief in a so-called divine reason—which fundamentalists have a hard time defending—is seen as superior to the use of our own reason. In this view, reason and belief are seen as two opposing forces. According to Tillich, however, we are better off developing a multidimensional understanding of religion that relies on all of our human faculties. At the top of this list is our ability to reason, and even to doubt. And because we have the power to reason, we must expect reasonable answers to our pressing questions, even if those answers are difficult or not the ones we want to hear.

To explain his approach to theology, Tillich developed what he calls the "method of correlation." This method of comprehending and explaining the Christian message is one of the reasons scholars characterize him as an "existential theologian." The method of correlation is a question-and-answer, dialogical encounter with ourselves and our existence. Using the insights of philosophy and psychology, we ask questions about the world, ourselves, and life's meanings. And in the process of analyzing existence in this way, we find that the Christian message and symbols provide answers to these questions and concerns. Through this method we find that religion is not blind obedience to centuries-old rules and commandments. Rather, religion is the always moving, collective response to eternal truths that are still applicable to our ever-changing world and lives.

One of the first things to notice about Tillich's method is that it stands in stark contrast to fundamentalism. Fundamentalism basically asks you to accept everything in the Bible on face value, even if what it says sometimes seems foreign to our experience, or somehow outdated or un-understandable. Tillich's method of correlation goes deeper than this by making the basic assumption that no words or teachings can be of true importance to us as humans unless they honestly answer the deep questions and difficulties we face in existence. Religion must address the innermost, universal questions of our hearts and minds. He sums up his existential method when he states that systematic theology

> makes an analysis of the human situation out of which the existential questions arise, and it demonstrates that the symbols used in the Christian message are the answers to these

> questions... Whenever man has looked at his world, he has found himself in it as a part of it. But he has also realized that he is a stranger in the world of objects, unable to penetrate it beyond a certain level of scientific analysis. And then he has become aware of the fact that he himself is the door to the deeper levels of reality, that in his own existence he has the only possible approach to existence itself.[9]

As you can see, Tillich's approach gives back to us our need for personal responsibility—the responsibility to question existence and to seek answers to the questions confronting us. Without this responsibility we become like automatons, lacking the desire or need to experience truth for ourselves. And if one's truth is not based on experience, but is simply the repetition of something handed down to us by tradition and blindly followed, then we haven't fully experienced what it means to be human. In the end, this also means we haven't experienced one of the central religious experiences: faith.

And this is a major part of the religious crisis today—people want simple answers to the complex questions about life. Unfortunately, this is just not possible. We are humans and we need to use our ability to reason; we can't simply believe stories about supernatural events from a distant era and call this "faith." Today, humanity's difficulty in believing miracle stories—when science and our experience tell us they are highly unlikely—is one of the main reasons religion is losing its relevance today. And this declining religious relevance comes from, as Tillich called it, the "lost dimension in religion," namely, the dimension of depth. Religion has largely made itself irrelevant by defining faith as the belief in miracle stories, and this is why we see modern cultures now rejecting this distorted concept of faith.

In 1958, in a famous essay published in the *Saturday Evening Post*, Tillich spoke of faith as "the state of being grasped by an infinite, or ultimate, concern." He then concluded that, by and large, most people in modern society have lost such a concern. And for the people who did still maintain an ultimate concern about something transcending their own limited, finite time and place in life, Tillich protested that many of these people were not being served by the historical religions of their time. As he put it, "It often happens that such people take the question of the meaning of their life infinitely seriously and reject any historical religion just for this reason. They feel that the concrete religions fail to express their profound concern adequately."[10] This fact is why many people today take issue with "organized" religion, and it's also why people will say they are "spiritual" but not "religious." In essence, "religion" has become a dirty word because what it represents in the modern age is so distorted from what it should be.

Many people critical of religion see it as a misguided human construct, or worse, as a controlling ideology created by humans and then imposed on the wider culture for purposes not always benevolent. In many instances this is a valid criticism, one Tillich often spoke of himself. This is why he says we sometimes have to reject ideas that have been passed down to us by family or religious authorities. That said, Tillich ultimately saw religion as a positive, fundamental reality inherent in the very fabric of our being—but only when it was expressed correctly. Like psychologist Carl Jung, Tillich saw religion as a potentially healing, or potentially destructive, force. Since neither Tillich nor Jung saw religion as a choice, but rather as a coming to terms with the religion-engendering forces within life, it was clear that how one viewed religion was of the utmost importance. Generally speaking, there are two ways to view religion; Tillich speaks of them in their "narrow" and "universal" expressions.

In the narrow expression, religion embodies a very particular set of beliefs, customs, rituals, or dogmas; such as in the case of Buddhism, Christianity, Confucianism, Hinduism, Judaism, Islam, etc. In the second, or wider, expression religion refers more generally to a mindset or disposition towards oneself and existence itself. Religion in this case is not confined to a particular belief system, but rather points to a state of concern one holds absolutely; in other words, it is an existential position concerning the nature of life itself. In this second sense, religion is universally human. It is a deep response to being alive, being conscious of having to die, and developing out of these facts a decided interest in *something*. Tillich refers to this as one having an Ultimate Concern; and this concern does not necessarily have to be defined in the narrow religious sense.

For instance, if one asks a mathematician, astronomer, or physicist how large the universe is, it's almost certain they will respond that it is infinite. If one then asks why they think this, they will respond that the laws of nature and scientific logic require it to be so. But ask them for a scientific proof to this and they will have no answer. Their own object of ultimacy, science itself, has yet to provide this proof. What, then, is the basis for their firm commitment to the notion that the universe is infinite? It is their absolute belief, their faith, if you will, in a universal, unchanging, and predictable logic to the laws that govern the universe. In following this logic to its end we would, as Stephen Hawking once said, know "the mind of God." And this is why Tillich claims that even so-called atheists have an Ultimate Concern, albeit not religious in the narrow sense of the word. Jung also expresses this sentiment when he states:

> Our sureness about material and physical phenomena is a mere illusion: we touch the surface of things but we know nothing about the inside. Naturally, science has discovered a number of methods that allow us to penetrate the secret to a certain extent; but the ultimate object is transcendent. It is beyond our grasp, simply because the nature by which we grasp, by which we attempt to understand consciousness or the psyche, is different from the object.[11]

Today, the failure of the Church to adequately express the meaning of its religious symbols is why it so often fails to remain relevant to peoples' lives, and thus why it has lost its "depth." In the end, Tillich claims there are two very specific ways humanity has lost the dimension of depth in religion or, said another way, "lost its faith": 1) an increasingly distorted relationship of humanity to others and the natural world and, 2) the literal interpretation of religious symbols and stories.

Speaking of the first distortion, Tillich says it's the scientific and technical control of nature—and modernity's objectifying and commodifying tendencies toward life itself—that cause us to lose sight of the depth of our existence. Using a spatial metaphor to illustrate this point, Tillich draws a distinction between the *horizontal* and *vertical* dimensions of life. He terms our obsession with frantically moving ahead in the horizontal dimension "forwardism," whereby we rarely stop to contemplate life's ultimate meaning—the vertical dimension. Here echoing the Buddhist notion that we must live in the moment to truly experience the depth of life, Tillich states:

> It [forwardism] runs ahead, every moment is filled with something which must be done or seen or said or planned. But no one can experience depth without stopping and becoming aware of himself. Only if he has moments in which he does not care about what comes next can he experience the meaning of this moment here and now and ask himself about the meaning of his life. As long as the preliminary, transitory concerns are not silenced. . . the voice of the ultimate concern cannot be heard. *This is the deepest root of the loss of the dimension of depth in our period—the loss of religion in its basic and universal meaning.*[12]

Aside from keeping us from resting in the moment and contemplating the depth and richness of life, living predominantly in the horizontal (finite, everyday) dimension has another negative consequence characteristic of modern life: the objectification of everything in existence, including nature and other humans. In economic terminology this is often referred to as the "commodification" of people and nature, and it is exemplified in the incessant capitalist drive to maximize profit at the expense of everything else. Because of this, the modern ecological crisis is one logical, though entirely unnecessary, expression of humanity's lost sight of life's depth.

Tillich concept of "forwardism" ties the loss of life's depth to our obsession with technology and constantly moving forward, without thinking or caring about the consequences such actions have. The dehumanization that comes with this led Tillich to call such a state of existence "demonic":

> I would say the most universal expression of the demonic today is a split between the control of nature by man and the fate of man to fall under the control of the product of his control. He produces, and then he falls under the power of what he has produced, the whole system of industrial existence. It has liberated him, it has given him control over nature and now it puts him into a servitude in which he loses more and more his being, his person.[13]

To many people today, the idea of living in a perfectly controlled, completely automated world is itself almost a religious vision. But Tillich would qualify this as "quasi-religious" obsession. It is quasi-religious, rather than truly religious, because it offers the technological "believer" an artificial feeling of self-transcendence—or elevation above the physical conditions of existence—into something seemingly meaningful and spiritually deep. However, by its very nature technology does not, in fact, deepen one's relationship to one's self, others, the world, or God (the Ground of Being). For this reason, Tillich posed a question decades ago that we commonly hear today: Is there a direct negative correlation between the advancement of technology and the quality of our relationships with each other and the world? As you might have guessed, Tillich's answer was a qualified "yes," for he did also see the positive benefits some technologies produce for humanity. He often pointed out the many technological advancements that have eased or eradicated immense suffering, as, for instance, in terms of human labor and human health (disease).

What Tillich wanted to emphasize with his concept of forwardism is the inherent problem of means and ends becoming confused in the development and use of technology. As we all know, technology is often pursued and developed simply because it can be. This is done without asking ourselves why we develop it, what consequences its usage will have on ourselves and the planet, or in what ways it may or may not deepen the meaning of our existence. The creation of nuclear weaponry—which could wipe humanity from the face of the earth—is a perfect example of this. A less devastating example is space travel. And Tillich uses this reality to sum up the concept of means-ends confusion:

> Space travel is a technical aim and somehow a technical possibility, but it is not determined by the organic needs of a living being. It is free, a matter of choice. However, this leads to a tension from which many conflicts of our contemporary culture arise: the perversion of the relation of means and ends by the unlimited character of technical possibilities. Means become ends simply because they are possible. But if possibilities become purposes only because they are possibilities, the genuine meaning of purpose is lost. Every possibility may be actualized. No resistance is forthcoming in the name of an ultimate end. The production of means becomes an end in itself, as in the case of the compulsive talker talking becomes an end in itself.[14]

Another great example of this is the push towards automating all aspects of our lives. Vast numbers of people would like to see us develop methods for controlling all the things in our life simply by thinking them, and not by actually having to say or do anything. This idea is not new, and it's been clearly expressed in many of the dystopian novels and films of this past century. They depict a life so technologically pre-planned and regulated that our humanity resembles nothing more than mindless automation and the quest for continual material satisfactions—often controlled by a central authoritarian government. The dehumanization accompanying such automation is the logical outcome of means-ends confusion, but the ultimate result is a loss of the human spirit and, with that, the depth of existence. Tillich sums it up well:

> The character of the human race in this state would be similar to what Nietzsche has described as the 'last man' who 'knows everything' and is not interested in anything. . . The negative utopias of our century, such as *Brave New World*, anticipate—rightly or wrongly—such a state of evolution.[15]

Decades before we took off on the path towards this type of dehumanized, synthetic existence, Tillich wrote of technology's disastrous and demonic effects on the human spirit and nature itself. This was truly groundbreaking, for he was the first theologian to make direct links between the ascendancy of technology and all its religious and ecological consequences. Since he was writing of these issues decades before the birth of the environmental movement—now characterized largely by talk of climate change, habitat loss, and rampant pollution—Tillich's assessment of this issue takes us deeper into understanding the depth of religion and the human spirit's need for an authentic experience of the natural world that sustains it. In that sense, his appreciation for nature is based on a genuine reverence for life, and not brought on because of the impending fear we now live with in our age of impending ecological crises.

His prescient religious sensitivity to this issue also explains why he so often spoke of us living in "the late stage of the self-destruction of industrial society, as a world above the given world of nature." In other words, we have created a "world" above the one given one, and now we are watching this human-created world fall down before our eyes—taking us and the rest of life with it:

> Man became increasingly able to control physical nature. Through the tools placed at his disposal by technical reason, he created a worldwide mechanism of large-scale production and competitive economy that began to take shape as a kind of 'second nature,' a Frankenstein, above physical nature and subjecting man to itself. While he was increasingly able to control and manipulate physical nature, man became less and less able to control his 'second nature.' He was swallowed up by his own creation. Step by step the whole of human life was subordinated to the demands of the new worldwide economy. Men became units of working power. The profit of the few and the poverty of the many were driving forces of the system.[16]

The second factor Tillich saw contributing to the loss of the depth dimension in religion is the misguided, but all-too-common, tendency of taking religious symbols and stories as literal. As we saw earlier, this was one of Tillich's main objection to fundamentalism. Fundamentalism fails to recognize that the Bible is not simply a collection of factual stories describing literal events that happened in the past, though this is obviously one element of the Bible. The Bible is a piece of literature composed of numerous literary forms the individual writers used to express deep human emotions and meanings: psalms, poems, epistles (letters), prophecies, gospels, parables, proverbs, oratory, etc.—to name a few. If these literary devices and the symbolisms they express are misunderstood and seen as literal stories, when they aren't meant to be, then all is lost:

> The first step toward the nonreligion of the Western world was made by religion itself. When it defended its great symbols, not as symbols, but as literal stories, it had already lost the battle. In doing so, the theologians... helped to transfer the powerful expressions of the dimension of depth into objects or happenings on the horizontal plane. There the symbols lose their power and meaning and become an easy prey to physical, biological and historical attack.[17]

There are two very specific stories from the Bible that have fallen prey to such literal interpretations: "Creation" and the "Fall" (Original Sin). In the quote below, take special note of Tillich's own interpretation of these two stories, as well as his use again of the spatial metaphor "horizontal"—the finite, everyday dimension of life. Using this metaphor, he highlights the distorting effect of taking religious symbols and interpreting them literally:

> If the symbol of creation which points to the divine ground of everything is transferred to the horizontal plane, it becomes a story of events in a removed past for which there is no evidence, but which contradicts every piece of scientific evidence. If the symbol of the Fall of Man, which points to the tragic estrangement of man and his world from their true being, is transferred to the horizontal plane, it becomes a story of a human couple a few thousand years ago in what is now present-day Iraq. One of the most profound psychological descriptions of the general human predicament becomes an absurdity on the horizontal plane.[18]

As we can see in this quote, Tillich hopes to point us toward a more realistic and truthful interpretation of the Bible. For example, the creation myth is distorted by saying that a divine being in a heavenly realm (God) literally created everything that exists in six days about 6,000 years ago. As Tillich will often point out, we know from scientific evidence this simply can't be true. And when fundamentalists insist that we accept this story as fact, they distort the meaning of faith and turn reasonable people away from the Christian message.

Regarding the story of the "Fall" (Original Sin), Tillich again debunks a literal interpretation of the Adam and Eve story by stating: "The notion of a moment in time in which man and nature were changed from good to evil is absurd, and it has no foundation in experience or revelation."[19] Or put another way: "The idea that the 'Fall' has physically changed the cellular or psychological structure of man (and nature?) is absurd and unbiblical."[20] Instead of viewing the story of the Fall literally, he says theology "must clearly and unambiguously represent 'the Fall' as a symbol for the human situation universally, and not as the story of an event that happened 'once upon a time.'"[21] In short, the Fall is a symbolic and mythical story that expresses humanity's "fall" away from what it should essentially be. It expresses the moral dilemma of having free choice and failing to always seek the truth, or do the good and the virtuous. In Tillich's terms, the story expresses the gap between our "existential self" and our "essential self."

Tillich goes on to explain how, during the Renaissance and Enlightenment periods, this idea that humans were somehow failing to become what they were supposed to be slowly faded away. Contrary to feeling estranged, or "fallen," humans now felt—however correctly or incorrectly—masters of their fate. Humanity started to develop a new sense of being in control of themselves and nature. For these periods of history, to stand firmly in everyday reality as it currently existed was not seen as a "fall"; instead, it was seen as a way to actualize one's potentialities and find perfection in existence. Science, philosophical rationalism, and the growing Western concept of progress were the defining characteristics of this time, and it gave humanity a new sense of human possibility. Vast and rapid advances in mathematics, science, and philosophy, as well as the development of more humane and democratic political systems, helped lessen the sense that humanity was, in fact, in some sort of moral decline. And no one could deny that humanity was, indeed, becoming more in control of its fate and evolving morally.

Unfortunately, history has shown that any sort of utopian thinking eventually finds itself thrown up against the sad reality of the darkness in human nature. And this is the basis of Tillich's constant distinction between our existential self and our essential self. To sum this distinction up we can say the following: because of our moral freedom and ability to reason, we have an acute awareness and experience of the negativities in life (anger, fear, guilt, judgment, pain, hate, spiritual emptiness, condemnation, etc.). We also sense that these negativities should be the opposite of what they are (joy, empathy, understanding, acceptance, tolerance, compassion, love). Because humans have an innate sense of this dichotomy—an internal conflict, if you will—they sense a moral responsibility for correcting these negativities. When we desire, and then move towards, overcoming the negative in our natures (existential distortion), and thus reach for the positive in our natures (essential actualization), we perform the moral act.

So to summarize the "Fall" we can say that, rather than a story of two people and a snake in a literal garden, it should instead be seen as a symbolic story of the human moral dilemma. Or, put in the form of a question: How do we decide between the conflicting choices our freedom permits us without increasing our estrangement from ourselves, others, the natural world, and ultimately God? In the end, Tillich's analyses of these two biblical stories show how the misinterpretation of myth can lead to major religious distortions. And what follows from these distortions is a loss of the "dimension of depth" in religion. This, in turn, often leads to a large-scale turning away from religion by reasonable people. And this is what we are seeing today.

Tillich's fascinating existential interpretation of these two stories is matched by his equally interesting, though rather simple, recommendation for how we get back the dimension of depth that such fundamentalist literalism has stolen. We don't get it back by increased church attendance or donations, renewed conversion, or by healing ceremonies. How do we get it then? According to Tillich, by stopping and realizing that we have lost it! In the very act of becoming aware that we have lost the dimension of depth, we actualize it: "He who realizes that he is separated from the ultimate source of meaning (God) shows by this realization that he is not only separated but also reunited."[22]

Having such a realization, and then changing who you are on the deepest level because of it, is exactly what being grasped by the dimension of depth means. It's the regaining of one's faith or, put another way, being grasped by a commitment and ultimate concern for something in our lives beyond the mere preliminary and transitory. But as Tillich always emphasized, in order to regain the dimension of depth we have to use our reason to see through the distortions forced upon us by fundamentalism, and not simply throw out all religion as a set of superstitious and outdated beliefs. And this brings us to the need for properly defining and understanding the realities of faith and God.

2

RE-IMAGINING FAITH AND GOD

> *"There are few words in the language of religion which cry for as much semantic purging as the word 'faith.' It is continually being confused with belief in something for which there is no evidence, or in something intrinsically unbelievable, or in absurdities and nonsense."*[23]

To the Christian fundamentalist, and unfortunately to the vast majority of the Western world, the word faith has come to mean a belief in statements lacking physical evidence. In fact, to many religious people the more unbelievable something is, the more worthy it is of the word faith. And this helps explain the importance many Christians place on the miracle stories of Jesus. However, to Tillich this is a complete misunderstanding of the word faith.

Properly understood, faith is an existential position regarding one's relationship to all of reality, and it is based on the total commitment of a person to whatever it is that concerns him or her ultimately. In this sense, faith is far more than belief, for it demands the complete involvement of a person—emotionally, intellectually, and morally. Faith, in other words, is not about believing the unbelievable; rather, it is a deep commitment to whatever it is that commands our Ultimate Concern—and in Christianity this would be a concern for love.

Because of this element of personal commitment, religious faith seeks truth in a way unlike that of science, even though it is not opposed to, or exclusive of, scientific truths. Tillich explains the nature of reason by contrasting two primary forms of it: scientific/technical/objective reason and participatory/ontological reason. Science seeks to distance itself from what it studies in order to understand the material *things* in the world; in that sense it produces objective and technical knowledge. Religion, on the other hand, concerns itself with understanding human *meanings* behind things; in that sense it is involved in its subject and produces participatory, ontological knowledge. While this is only a general description of the ways we learn and know things, it's important to emphasize that a scientist is not necessarily unconcerned about larger religious or ethical issues beyond scientific facts. Nor does it mean a religious person is necessarily unconcerned about scientific facts and how the world works. American philosopher and psychologist, William James, sums this up well:

> Science gives to all of us telegraphy, electric lighting, and diagnosis, and succeeds in

> preventing and curing a certain amount of disease. Religion... gives to some of us serenity, moral poise, and happiness, and prevents certain forms of disease as well as science does, or even better in a certain class of persons. Evidently, then, the science and the religion are both of them genuine keys for unlocking the world's treasure-house to him who can use either of them practically. Just as evidently neither is exhaustive or exclusive of the other's simultaneous use.[24]

Tillich continually reminds us that science and religion should never be in conflict, as they operate in different dimensions of human experience. But the element of commitment inherent in religious faith means there is a dangerous risk to it—specifically, idolatry:

> The risk of faith is that it could affirm a wrong symbol of ultimate concern, a symbol which does not really express ultimacy (as, e.g., Dionysus or one's nation). But this risk lies in quite a different dimension from the risk of accepting uncertain historical facts... The risk of faith is existential; it concerns the totality of our being, while the risk of historical judgments is theoretical and open to permanent scientific correction. Here are two different dimensions which should never be confused.

> A wrong faith can destroy the meaning of one's
> life; a wrong historical judgment cannot.[25]

For example, if I place my faith—my Ultimate Concern—into my nation and support every act it commits with the totality of my being, only to find out later that it was involved in horrible atrocities against humanity, what then? Such idolatrous, misplaced faith can shatter the understanding of my existence, or existence in general. In drastic cases, it can also bring about an existential crisis and reduce my desire or ability to find a faith that is sound and viable.

This inherent danger for faith to become idolatrous is why Tillich says doubt is a healthy element in any expression of faith. And let's face it, being the fallible humans we are, there are many, many things we cannot know with absolute certainty. Sadly, this doesn't stop millions of people from claiming to know things with absolute certainty, as we see in all forms of fundamentalist religion. But as we also know, the psychological consequence of this type of thinking usually results in a rigid, dogmatic, anti-rational, and judgmental personality. This is why the fundamentalist repression of doubt is one of its most dangerous elements, for it cuts off a vital and useful part of us—our ability to question, reason, and change our views based on evidence and experience. But in order to achieve any of these, one has to accept the fact that doubt is an inescapable, in fact healthy, part of existence.

Doubt is something Tillich wrote extensively about, and he characterizes it as having two primary expressions. The first kind of doubt he calls cynical, or skeptical, doubt. The second type is radical, or existential, doubt. Using his earlier horizontal-vertical metaphor, we can say that skeptical doubt is only concerned with the horizontal (everyday, finite) dimension of life. This would include doubt about scientific, economic, historical, or political theories, for example. We understand this type of doubt as healthy, natural, and necessary in these realms, for it's how we gain solid objective knowledge of the world.

But for many religious people of a fundamentalist bent, the second type, radical or existential doubt, is seen as a threat to one's faith. This is because existential doubt requires a participation of the whole person in whatever it doubts—leaving one open to the possibility of deep questions or doubts about one's beliefs. Skeptical doubt in scientific and economic matters, for example, does not require this participation. So in the following quote from Tillich we can see why so many religious people are scared of, and therefore repress, any doubt they may have: "Radical doubt is existential doubt concerning the meaning of life itself; it may include not only the rejection of everything religious in the narrow sense of the word but also the ultimate concern which constitutes religion in the larger sense."[26] In short, one's doubt may even threaten one's deeply held traditional religious beliefs.

But this is the risk that must be taken. Why? Because in the end, doubt and reason also help us determine what is and what is not, in fact, worthy of our ultimate concern. It keeps us from idolatry, as well as from falling prey to belief in supernatural religious theories that just don't make sense. And without reason, humans are likely to believe just about anything—one of the reasons so many modern, rational people find religion irrelevant, outdated, or even ridiculous.

In the next chapter, we will cover the various forms of reason and why reason is a vital part of faith. It will then become clear why the commonly held belief that reason is the enemy of religion is built on a misunderstanding of what faith and religion actually are. But now that we have a basic understanding of how Tillich understands faith, it's necessary to explore his ideas on the reality that faith is directed to, namely, God.

God

"It is as atheistic to affirm the existence of God as it is to deny it. God is being-itself, not a being."[27]

Whenever I have a conversation with someone and they say they don't believe in God—which is quite common these days—I always ask which God they don't believe in. I've found the answers are strikingly similar. Whether talking about the Christian, Muslim, or Judaic God, the answers always come down to disbelief in the existence of a being standing outside the world, judging us, and changing the course of natural events at will. And to this protestation against God existing as a being or thing, Tillich is in total agreement. To Tillich, this idea of God is not only unbiblical, it is also logically impossible and damaging to Christian faith.

The idea of God not being a thing, person, or being is a massive stumbling block for most people, Christian or not. We are so accustomed to thinking of God as a being or person that to posit anything else just seems odd or inconceivable. And this is a primary reason the modern discussion between science and religion is so misguided and stunted; both sides share a common misconception of God. Both see religion as the human attempt to establish a relationship with a divine being that exists in a realm of reality we cannot see or know in a tangible way. Tillich summarizes the problem from both sides of this mistakenly-framed debate:

> It is just this idea of religion which makes any understanding of religion impossible. If you start with the question whether God does or does not exist, you can never reach Him; and if you assert that He does exist, you can reach Him even less than if you assert that he does not exist. A God whose existence or nonexistence you can argue is a thing beside others within the universe of existing things. . . It is regrettable that scientists believe that they have refuted religion when they rightly have shown that there is no evidence whatsoever for the assumption that such a being exists. Actually, they have not only not refuted religion, but they have done it a considerable service. They have forced it to reconsider and to restate the meaning of the tremendous word God. Unfortunately, many theologians make the same mistake. They begin their message with the assertion that there is a highest being

> called God, whose authoritative revelations they have received. They are more dangerous for religion than the so-called atheistic scientists. They take the first step on the road which inescapably leads to what is called atheism. Theologians who make of God a highest being who has given some people information about Himself, provoke inescapably the resistance of those who are told they must subject themselves to the authority of this information.[28]

All of us probably grew up learning that God is a man in the sky who decides what will and will not happen in the universe. Unfortunately, as Tillich points out, this belief is detrimental to people trying to understand religion. And this is why he was out to destroy the idea once and for all.

To explain God, Tillich relied on the Christian mystical (Platonic) tradition describing ultimate reality with the philosophical concept of *Being*. As Tillich explains it, the problem with making God into a thing, being, or person is that it takes something that is supposed to be the foundation and structure of all reality and makes it, instead, a part of that reality. So this is why Tillich calls God the "Ground of Being," rather than *a* being. He explains it this way:

> Since God is the ground of being, he is the ground of the structure of being. He is not subject to this structure; the structure is grounded in him. He *is* this structure, and it is impossible

to speak about him except in terms of this structure.[29]

Once we have grasped the concept of being and understand why it's incorrect to make God into an object—even a "highest" object—we begin to understand a lot of the problematic issues in contemporary religion. We also begin to see why so many people reject this idea of God as a being or person; such a conception means God is external to the world instead of being the basis of the world:

> The being of God is being-itself. The being of God cannot be understood as the existence of a being alongside or above others. If God is *a* being, he is subject to the categories of finitude, especially to space and substance. Even if he is called the 'highest being' in the sense of the 'most perfect' and 'the most powerful' being, this situation is not changed... They place him on the level of other beings while elevating him above all of them. Many theologians who have used the term 'highest being' have known better.[30]

This is why Tillich says that the only literal, non-symbolic statement we can make about God is that God is *Being-Itself*. All other statements, such as God is "all-knowing," or God is "love," are symbolic. And this is what led to his formulation that God, properly understood, is our Ultimate Concern. What he means by this is that the reality of God—the Ground and structure of Being—is so overwhelmingly important and significant that our relationship to this dimension of life qualifies all other earthly concerns as temporal, transitory, or relatively insignificant. Or said another way, in the midst of life's threats and our insecurities and doubts about it—existential anxiety, guilt, estrangement, disease, and meaninglessness—only God can be the foundation for our existence that is not altered by the changing conditions of life. In this sense,

> 'God' is the answer to the question implied in man's finitude; he is the name for that which concerns man ultimately. This does not mean that first there is a being called God and then the demand that man should be ultimately concerned about him. It means that whatever concerns a man ultimately becomes god for him, and, conversely, it means that a man can be concerned ultimately only about that which is god for him.[31]

God, in other words, is the word used to describe the reality giving existence its ultimate meaning. And since love is the human experience we feel as so overwhelmingly meaningful that it eclipses all other human realities, Tillich said this gives a foundation to the symbolic statement "God is love." Therefore, when love is the aim of our lives and love characterizes our relationships with others and the world itself, then we can say that God is living within us, and we are living within God. In the Christian mystical tradition, this is described as us participating in God.

To reiterate, Tillich says that since God is the very ground and structure of all reality, it's pointless to say that God exists. It's like trying to argue that gravity or love exists; there is no need to say this, as we know they do from experience. They do not exist in the literal, physical sense, but we experience them nonetheless. If we understand God as the very structure of existence, then we are in the same situation—the need to say that God exists or does not exist is no longer there.

Sadly, many Christians desperately want to prove that God exists as a being out there in the universe because, often quite self-consciously, they think their faith stands or falls on this proof. But, as Tillich points out, we cannot possibly prove the existence of God anyway. In order to prove something, it must first exist. On the other hand, every atheist wants to prove God doesn't exist so they can finally overcome having to hear about what they see as an infantile belief in some Man in the Sky. Unfortunately, both sides are simply wrong to argue for or against the existence of God. So let me explain in the shortest, simplest way I can why we must stop talking about whether God exists or not.

To say someone is an *atheist* means they don't believe in a thing, or being, called God. On the other hand, to be a *theist* means you do believe in the existence of a thing, or being, called God. In listening to people talk, it would seem these are the only two options we are left with. But there is a middle way that avoids these two limited, misguided options. That middle way—Tillich's way—points out that God should not been understood as a being or thing at all; not even the highest being or thing. Rather, God is *Being-Itself*—the very ground and structure of everything that exists. And again, Tillich says this is the only literal, or non-symbolic, thing we can say about God. Which brings us to the concept of symbols and why they are so important to understand, particularly in regards to the religious dimension of human life.

According to Tillich, a symbol is something that opens up another dimension of reality to us that would otherwise not be known. Symbols are often used in religion, but there are also many other uses for them. For example, on a political level a nation's flag expresses something that cannot be fully explained with just words, even with the use of words such as freedom, democracy, or justice. In science we use symbolic images or words to describe some things we cannot even see, but know are there because of the force exert. And in religion we use symbolic terms to describe God, such as "omniscient" (all-knowing) and "omnipresent" (everywhere at once); but these statements are not meant to be taken literally. And the danger of taking religious symbols literally is what Tillich fought so fiercely against.

When taken literally, religious symbols can become absurd. For example, how can one individual being—even a so-called divine being called God—be everywhere at once? It's logically impossible. Another example is when people say God is the "Father" of Jesus. This is obviously a symbolic statement, for to take it literally is to fall prey to an illogical, supernatural belief; if God is not a human, then how can he literally be the father of Jesus? Again, these examples show the problem with fundamentalist understandings of God and the universe; they take symbolic statements and literalize them. And when they do this, they make absurd supernatural statements that run counter to logic. In turn, this lack of logic causes people to see all religion as ridiculous or meaningless.

However, if we grasp the symbolic nature of religious language, we can begin to see the proper way to understand and express the reality this language seeks to describe. For example, I mentioned previously how love might not be a physical reality we can see and touch, but it is nonetheless a symbolic word that points to something we know as "real." We could say the same about the words "mind," "time," or even "life." Though we use these words on a daily basis, we still cannot say we fully understand their meaning or their workings. We understand what the words mean to us, and we have no trouble throwing them around as if they are fully understood realities, but we know the reality is so much more than words can touch. Even biology, one of the most well understood branches of modern science, cannot explain the full complexity, workings, and implications of the term life; even the very nature of bodily healing is still not fully understood.

What I hope to show from all these examples is that a symbol is something of human meaning or value that we can experience, regardless of whether it has objective, or material, reality. For example, think of the symbols in a powerful dream or a work of art, evoking certain inexplicable feelings in us which we experience, but to which we cannot put words. And whether we are the creator or observer, this is why humans create art—to access to a dimension of our humanity that all the scientific discoveries and philosophies in the world simply cannot touch or explain.

The problem with symbols is that when we say something is a symbol, people often think something is "only a symbol" and, therefore, is not "real." This comes from science's strong influence over how we understand and define reality; something is real only if it has physical properties we can see, touch, and study on the physical level. This circumscribed understanding of reality can be termed physicalism, scientism, and/or materialist reductionism, wherein reality is reduced to only the physical and chemical—only matter "matters." When we get to the chapter on reason we'll see that such a view is only one way we can understand and explain the world; it is a vital way, but it is not the only valid way. Let me use an analogy to describe how we might begin to more accurately think and speak about God.

As I mentioned before, there are two realities, amongst many others, that we know exist, even though they don't have any physical properties that we can see and touch: love and gravity. I don't know of a single sane human who would deny the reality of these two things. But I also don't know a single human who would say they "exist," in the sense that they are material things to be seen and touched. This is how we need to begin thinking about God—as something we know from experience, but which cannot be seen as existing in some physical way.

The Swiss psychologist, Carl Jung, follows this line of thought when he says that God is a "psychological fact." And Tillich would agree with this assessment, for both of them see religion as an innate dimension of our humanity. The trouble is that humanity has fallen short in understanding and describing this reality. For some people, the awareness of the religious dimension of life only comes in times of deep existential crises, such as a diagnosis of cancer or a near-death experience. Or, on a societal level, the religious dimension might be experienced when humanity threatens the world's ecological stability and this, in turn, begins to threaten our own health and/or existence. Or it might happen with the imminent threat of nuclear annihilation.

As finite beings, we endure personal and societal threats that we know will one day culminate in the end of our lives, and this is unsettling, to say the least. But these threats can also bring about an awareness of being part of something that transcends our own ego or limited place in history; in other words, if open to the experience, they can reveal something eternal in our consciousness and being. And this feeling of belonging to something beyond our own egos and limited place in time and space brings about a sense that, beyond death, we may return to this reality from which we came. This is a key feature of religious feelings, or consciousness, and Tillich characterizes it as our desire to return to God, the Ground of our very being.

Theologians and philosophers for centuries have tried to argue for or against the existence of God. Some have argued that God must exist because God is a "necessary thought" when we contemplate the complexity of the world (St. Anselm). Other arguments see God as the First Cause at the end of a long process of argumentation when we ask where the world came from. Or God is seen as the intelligence driving the universe toward its ultimate fulfillment.

Then there's the "God of the gaps" argument, whereby gaps in our scientific knowledge are used as proof that God exists; if we can't explain the origins or basis of something, then this must prove the existence of some supernatural being at work in the universe. In this logic, lack of scientific evidence for what caused the creation of the universe is seen as proof that God created it, for what else could explain the existence of a complex life form like us? This very unsophisticated argument recently led Pope Francis to come out and proclaim that "God is not a magician," a point Tillich often made himself. Thus, according to Tillich and the Pope, the Big Bang and evolutionary theory should not be opposed, because all the evidence points to them being sound theories.

For Tillich, there are no arguments or proofs for the existence of God. Does this mean the idea of God is unnecessary or wrong? No. Again, it's just the way we've understood and talked about God that is wrong. But for all their shortcomings, to Tillich these arguments are, nonetheless, correct expressions of the religious dimension to human life: "The arguments for the existence of God analyze the human situation in such a way that the question of God appears possible and necessary. The question of God is possible because an awareness of God is present in the question of God. This awareness precedes the question."[32]

As I pointed out earlier, to both Tillich and Jung God is innate in the human experience itself. The problem arises when we misconceive of what God is, or when we try to make God into a thing or being. And this is the problem all the so-called arguments have in common—*they still speak of God as a thing.* Tillich again: "God does not exist. He is being-itself beyond essence and existence. Therefore, to argue that God exists is to deny him."[33] That's a pretty strong, controversial statement coming from one of the world's most respected theologians, but it is effective in pointing to the problem of thinking of God as a thing or being.

Many famous opponents of the idea of God—such as Sigmund Freud and Karl Marx, to name just two—claim that God is simply a projection of human wishes, human characteristics, or infantile human fantasies created to cope with the difficulties of our existences.[34] In some cases, Tillich would agree with this assessment. The only difference is that Tillich didn't "throw the baby out with the bath water." In other words, Tillich saw the distortions in religion, but he also recognized that, if correctly understood and expressed, religion was a healthy, natural, and necessary outcome of the human encounter with reality. So while he remained deeply indebted to both Marx and Freud, he was also highly critical of the limitations of their theories.

For Tillich, both figures analyzed human existence in very significant ways, Marx in the economic and political realms and Freud in psychology. Ironically, though both Freud and Marx were staunchly antireligious, Tillich insisted that some of their theories contributed to a more authentic religious outlook. They did this by stripping back the false ideologies humans had created to hide the deeper, more rational truths of existence.

Analyzing political and economic factors, Marx unveiled the ways an elite power class (the bourgeoisie) kept the majority of humans in a state of poverty, alienation, and dehumanization. As such, Tillich's own early involvement in Religious Socialism relied heavily on Marx's insights into the demonic nature of capitalism. It also caused Tillich to see Marx as a prophetic force due to his demand and expectation of a more just and humane society, a society defined by economic justice and equality. In the end, this led to Tillich's paradoxical—and, to some, heretical—statement that Marx was one of the greatest theologians who ever existed.

Tillich, who was well-versed and very interested in depth psychology, also saw Freud's insights into the inner workings of the psyche as contributing to a better understanding of religion. Through psychoanalysis, we can unveil the hidden, unconscious impulses and fears that often drive humans into self-delusion and increased alienation from themselves, others, and society. This opens up the potential for humans to lead a more authentic life, one in which their essential self is increasingly revealed. So while Freud thought he had discredited religion with his discoveries, Tillich took many of his insights to quite other conclusions. This was especially the case concerning Freud's theory of projection. In fact, Tillich turned Freud's theory of God as a projection upside down when he pointed out that even though every image of God is, on some level, a projection from within the human being, we have to recognize that

> projection always is projection *on* something—
> a wall, a screen, another being, another realm...

> The realm against which the divine images are projected is not itself a projection. It is the experienced ultimacy of being and meaning. It is the realm of ultimate concern.[35]

Simply put, when Tillich speaks here metaphorically of a screen or realm "against which the divine images are projected," he is not speaking of a divine being named God that Freud had in mind when he tried to discredit religion as nothing but the projection of a human created image. No, Tillich is not speaking of anything material "out there" in the universe at all, i.e., a being called God. Rather, Tillich is speaking of this screen in existential terms as our internal experience of the depth, meaning, and ultimacy of our existence. This sense of an Ultimate Concern—directed at something transcendent to our individual being—is a reality that both draws this concern out of us, as well as the reality this concern is directed towards.

When we conceive of God, something *is* actually being projected. The problem is that we are limited in our ability to adequately express in imagery what the source of this experience is, i.e., what God is. But what Tillich is sure of is that what we project comes from a very real sense of ultimacy—something unique to the human species. This is why, as an existentialist, for Tillich all things religious or spiritual are—before anything else—rooted in the immediacy and depth of our human experience.

What we experience as human ultimacy in the experience of God is as real as anything—as real as gravity or love, for example. But we have to use symbolic images and words that limit this actual lived experience. So when we say God is Father, God is wise, or God is love, we are simply projecting—in a symbolic way—our very real psychological experiences of feeling 1) cared for when we are in need of protection, 2) in need of wisdom when lost or confused, or 3) being loved in an ultimate, unconditional way. But far too often we have distorted this experience, this reality, by making God into an external thing "out there" that must exist in a material way. And that is why symbols are often inadequate or can lead to something logically absurd—such as God as a bearded man in the sky. In short, when we take the existential experience that we call "religious" and try to literalize it, or make an abstraction out of it, that's when we run into problems understanding religion. Tillich, Freud, and Marx all understood this.

Even though Tillich completely disagreed with Freud's outright dismissal of religion and his theory of religious projection, he still hailed his discovery of the unconscious realm of the human psyche as monumental to the advancement of religion. As I mentioned before, this discovery brought to light a deeper dimension of the psyche not previously known, and this had great significance for our understanding of reality itself. For instance, Freud's theories and practice—along with Jung and many others who study the psyche—helped us understand that consciousness is not reducible to strictly biological or chemical processes. In other words, human psychology, as well as the world itself, is not explicable in only physical, material terms; there is a depth to reality scientific understanding cannot touch. Tillich seized on this discovery and then pushed it to its logical conclusion:

> If we enter the levels of personal existence which have been rediscovered by depth psychology, we encounter the past, the ancestors, the collective unconscious, the living substance in which all living beings participate. In our search for the "really real" we are driven from one level to another to a point where we cannot speak of level any more, where we must ask for that which is the ground of all levels, giving them their structure and their power of being.[36]

At the very depth of the human psyche is a personal experience of God—whether we call it by that name or not. But what about when people say God is "personal"? The most important answer Tillich gives to this question is: "'Personal God' does not mean God is *a* person. It means that God is the ground of everything personal... He is not personal, but he is not less than personal."[37] This can sound confusing, but basically what Tillich is saying is that humans cannot be concerned ultimately about something impersonal, or something that is just another object, and this is where the symbol of "personal God" comes from. As we've already seen, God is not a person for Tillich, and thus the term personal God is another symbolic term we use to describe our experience of the depth and ground of our existence.

In 1940, Albert Einstein gave a lecture outlining his criticisms of the idea of a personal God. Tillich then delivered a response to it, agreeing with some points but challenging others. Tillich made the basic point we covered earlier: the concept of a being called God interfering with, or being a cause of, natural events, makes God into a thing or a being. According to Tillich, no criticism of this distorted idea of God can be sharp enough.[38] For this reason, Tillich liked to speak of God as "suprapersonal" instead of "personal." As such, God is not a person, but God is also more than our experience of personhood. In the experience of God, we are driven out of our personal egos and into a concern for humanity and the world as a whole. Again, this is why we say, symbolically, that God is love. When we are driven to love another person, or life, or our experience of the world itself, we experience the "personhood" of God in those encounters.

Even though Tillich was critical of the term personal God, in some respects he still saw this symbol as indispensable to religion. Why? Because the most direct concern we can have in existence is for another person. Said another way, the most direct experience we have of God is through the love of another person. Tillich expresses this in the following quote, but ends it by pointing out how our Ultimate Concern must transcend even this human-to-human encounter of love:

> The more concrete a thing is, the more possible concern about it. The completely concrete being, the individual person, is the object of the most radical concern—the concern of love. On the other hand, ultimate concern must transcend every preliminary finite and

> concrete concern. It must transcend the whole realm of finitude in order to be the answer to the question implied in finitude... This is the inescapable inner tension in the idea of God.[39]

In short, concern for another human is a gateway to an immediate experience of God; and it is when we love another person that we most experience the reality of a "personal" God. But that said, no matter how much we love them or they love us, another human can't be the ultimate answer to the problems of existence, precisely because existence itself is the problem. Therefore, the answers to our problems in existence must, in a sense, come from beyond a merely human encounter. This is the foundation for understanding Tillich's idea of God as the answer to the ultimate questions of our existence.

Tillich agreed that no arguments can prove there is a being called God. Regardless, humans will continue to seek for and speak about this reality. This is because we have an internal understanding and experience of what God is through our sense of morality. We understand and reach God when we actualize our essential self in the moral act; sensing our limitations and our failure to be who we should be, we seek to become what we "ought" to be.

Tillich describes how in this awareness of our need to be something more—our need to actualize our "essential self," as opposed to our distorted "existential self"— the question of God arises: "If he [the human] were what he essentially is, if his potentiality were identical with his actuality, the question of the infinite [God] would not arise." This goes back to the basic Tillichian point I emphasized at the very beginning of this book: Humans are estranged in all the dimensions of their existence—from themselves (psychological dimension), from others (social dimension), from nature (ecological/material dimension), and from God (spiritual dimension). Though estranged, we seek for healing and reunion with these various dimensions of existence. The striving for reunion with all dimensions of reality—the striving for our essential, or true, self—is the reason religion exists. As long as humans sense they are not what they are supposed to be, but strive to discover and become it, religion will be with us. And we find religion serving its purposes correctly when, however fragmentarily, our essential self shines through the distortions of our existing self.

In many ways, this resonates with Buddhist teachings on the self. In fact, when he sums up an experience of the religious dimension of life, one Zen master's thoughts are shockingly close to Tillich's own concept of God and faith:

> To exist in big mind [Tillich: *our essential self*] is an act of faith, which is different from the usual faith of believing in a particular idea or being. It is to believe that something is supporting us and supporting all our activities including thinking mind and emotional feelings. All these things are supported by something big that has no form or color. It is impossible to know what it is, but something exists there,

> something that is neither material nor spiritual. Something like that always exists, and we exist in that space. That is the feeling of pure being [Tillich: *God*].[40]

In other words, we are grounded in, and supported by, an infinitely rich dimension of being to which we belong, but from which we are estranged. This reality continually calls for us to become what we are intended to be. And in becoming what we are intended to be, our life experiences and relationships with others, ourselves, and the planet deepens. This process—this continual choice between doing what will help us overcome estrangement and become what we are intended to be—is the moral act.

When it's all said and done, in part we come to experience and understand God like the earlier philosophers and theologians did—through reason. But, you might ask, isn't this a contradiction since Tillich says you cannot prove the existence of God with reason? Don't we really know God through faith, which is the opposite of reason? Well, you'll recall that faith is only the opposite of reason if we think faith means believing in something that can't be proven by reason—a definition of faith we dispelled at the beginning of the book. Faith *does* use reason, only it's a different type of reason. With that said, let's now look at Tillich's understanding of reason and how it helps us understand and relate to God.

3

REASON AS ESSENTIAL TO RELIGION

If we're to understand what reason is, and why it's so important if we're to grasp the nature of religion, we first have to understand the different types of reason. For Tillich, there are two primary forms, but he uses several terms to describe depending on the context. First, there is a reason he calls technical, objective, controlling, or scientific. And then there is subjective, participatory, or ontological reason. To simplify things, I'll use "technical reason" hereafter for the former and "ontological reason" for the latter.

Basically, technical reason helps us understand the material, scientific questions of the world (the who, what, where, and when questions). Ontological reason helps us understand the basic "why" questions of our existence. Tillich likes to call ontological reason the "depth of reason," for it penetrates below the surface level of most scientific reasoning in its search for answers to questions science cannot answer.

The ancient philosophical and biblical concept of *logos* helps illustrate this second form of reason. *Logos* is the root suffix for reason/knowledge, and it's used when describing the study of various forms of reality: bio-logy, psych-ology, physi-ology, etc. But the concept points to something much larger than just the study of things, and this is why it was adopted by Christianity. Bart Ehrlich, a religious historian, sums *logos* up well concerning ancient Greek philosophy:

> Stoics believed that Logos—reason—was a divine element that infused all of existence. There is, in fact, a logic to the way things are, and if you want to understand this world—and more important, if you want to understand how best to live in this world—then you will seek to understand its underlying logic. . . [T]his is possible because Logos is not only inherent in nature, it resides in us as human beings. We ourselves have a portion of Logos given to us, and when we apply our minds to the world, we can understand it. If we understand the world, we can see how to live in it.[41]

Understood in this light, reason and knowledge are seen as virtues, where reason is gained and used not only to cognitively understand things, but to also learn how to *be* in the world in a moral sense. Thus, we see *logos* used in its biblical form when Jesus is described as the *Logos* ("Word") itself, notably in the Gospel of John. When *logos* is used in this way it expresses the idea not that Jesus has knowledge of everything, but rather, that in his being and person the ultimate logic and reason of human existence is made manifest, i.e., Jesus' life and actions show us how to *be* in relation to others and the world.

In this classic philosophical and biblical usage of the term we see ontological reason expressed, because *Logos* points to a way of understanding the world that is deeper than the reason we use to study and understand things objectively. So broadly speaking, while we can discover scientific truths through technical reason, we can discover and understand religion, morality, human emotions, symbolism, psychology, history, and many other things, through ontological reason.

We can, of course, use technical reason to study the physical and chemical foundations of the mind and emotions, as in cognitive science. But ultimately, technical reason is limited to explaining structures and processes in the material world, rather than their phenomenological or existential significance to the person, or persons, experiencing them. Technical reason requires us to distance ourselves from our object of study in order to understand it better, whereas ontological reason can be seen as quite different than this—and that's why Tillich also calls it "objective" reason. Ontological, or subjective, reason denotes a type of reason where we are committed to, or participate in, what it is we are studying.

Before we see these two forms of reason as inherently conflicting with each other, it must be said that technical reason and ontological reason are two parts of a unified whole—both valid, but only when used in their proper dimensions. And this point underscores why all the arguments for the existence of

God fall flat; as discussed earlier, what each of the arguments does is bring God down to the level of earthly objects, or of cause-effect relationships, within the world. In other words, the arguments for the existence of God use technical reason to try and discover something that can only be approached through ontological reason since, as Tillich always explains, God is Being-Itself, not *a* being. For instance, the arguments for the existence of God use technical reason to make God into a being or person who chooses to do some things and not others. But a God who decides for one thing and not another is a limited, misconceived God. Tillich even goes so far as to say that a God who did decide in this way could be seen as evil, and this is the logic most people use (quite correctly) when pointing out that a God who lets one person live and another die prematurely, or in a painful way, is not worthy of being revered or worshipped.

Technical reason helps us see that God cannot logically be a person, let alone a person choosing to do one thing and not another. This would make God limited in some sense. Rather, as the Ground of all Being, God is best understood as the very foundation, or structure, of existence. Scientists such as Stephen Hawking and Albert Einstein have spoken similarly of God as an ultimate "intelligence" that forms the structure of existence. Seen this way, God is what sustains everything that exists and, therefore, cannot be apart from anything that exists.

Because Tillich does not believe God is a separate being or thing, but rather is the structure of all being, many people have tried to claim that he's not Christian but is instead a pantheist (where God is literally "in" existing things, such as a tree). But this assessment of him is mistaken. Tillich always emphasizes that God, though the Ground of all that exists, still transcends the world and therefore cannot be equated with it. This is important to emphasize because many Christians believe there is a danger in seeing God "in" things. When one does this, according to such arguments, then one is likely to worship the things in the world rather than God. Of course, this is a simplistic understanding of reality and leads to an unnecessary anti-nature stance. One should be able to have love of the world (creation) and love of God; they are not mutually exclusive experiences.

Tillich's answer to this conflict is to say that, rather than envision God as a separate object or being altering the course of events in the world, we should instead see God as "acting" creatively through each being's nature: biologically, psychologically, historically, and spiritually through humans; organically through plants and animals; and inorganically through rocks, for example. Thus, using a spatial metaphor, Tillich sees God working in and through nature and humanity organically from the ground up. Fundamentalism, on the other hand, sees God as an object or power above us, forcing events in this or that way. In other words, fundamentalists see God as a completely foreign, authoritative power connected with us in a supernatural way: creating us, rewarding or punishing us based on our actions, and then judging us when we die.

While Tillich would be the first to point out technical reason's inability to grasp the symbol and reality of God— precisely because it tries to understand God as a thing or being—he is also the first to point out technical reason's incredible ability to destroy superstitions. This might include science's ability to undermine distorted conceptions of God as a rewarder or punisher, or misguided ideas on how old the earth is, or stories in the Bible like Noah's Ark which fly in the face of how we know the world works. Therefore, Tillich says theology should always be grateful for technical reason. However, trying to use technical reason to understand religion is where problems arise.

Tillich sums up the limitations of technical reason when he states that it "has given a tremendous preponderance to the side of detachment. What cannot be grasped by analytic reasoning is relegated to emotion. All the relevant problems of existence are thrown out of the realm of knowledge into the formless realm of emotion. Assertions about the meaning of life and the depth of reason are denied any truth value."[42] What Tillich touches on here is the common scientific attack that religion is merely an emotional experience lacking any objective validity. The basic answer to this critique is the following: even if our emotions could be explained right down to every single physical and chemical reaction within the body, would this even begin to touch on our actual *experience* of the emotion? Isn't our experience of something larger and richer than a scientific explanation of it? This is why Tillich called materialism an "ontology of death":

> If the whole of reality is reduced to inorganic processes, the result is the non-scientific ontological theory which is called materialism or

> reductionist naturalism. Its peculiar contention is not that there is matter in everything that exists—every ontology must say this including all forms of positivism—but that the matter we encounter under the dimension of the inorganic is the only matter.[43]

These big questions regarding knowledge and reason cause Tillich to make an interesting observation about the scientific tendency to place abstraction over direct, lived experience, thus missing the creative act of living because of the estrangement such abstraction causes within us. In the following quote, you can see the problems that arise when we try to make concepts, symbols, and experiences into material things, whether they be "God" or "electrons":

> In the act of knowledge, the element of detachment becomes overwhelming. The subject separates itself from the object in order to know it. And in this way a 'second world,' so to speak, is created by man, the world of known objects, what we call the 'objective' world. It is not the world as we encounter it, as we encounter it in every moment in which we look at it. But is a world that is constructed by man's cognitive power, by his ability to observe, and to abstract, and to create concepts, and to create laws. It is very interesting that modern physicists are very much aware of the fact that their most abstract

> concepts are their own creations. The electron is a valid concept. You can destroy mankind and perhaps the whole earth with the knowledge that is given to us by the discovery of the electron. But the electron the physicists know is not an object, a thing beside other things. So we must distinguish, even in physics where the detached attitude is most outspoken, a valid concept from an object, from a thing.
>
> And so it is generally. The world of objects is a construct of man's mind, nevertheless a valid construct.[44]

With all this said about the limits of technical reason, Tillich still always points out that technical, scientific arguments are essential for undercutting religious ideas that run counter to valid scientific theories and/or laws. Nonetheless, technical reason cannot touch the reality of faith. Why? Because faith is not about proving something that seems improvable—even the existence of a being called God. This is the distorted concept of faith; faith is an existential position, a commitment to something in which you participate, and for which you have an allegiance or love. And because every healthy-minded person has some ultimate truth they hold, however hidden or unconscious it might be, Tillich claims there is no such thing as an atheist.

So to really understand Tillich's concept of faith and reason you have to ask yourself: What is the reality on which I ultimately rely? What is it in my life that I am not willing to abandon, forsake, or live without? Is there some principle that is ultimate to me? Is it Truth, Creativity, Virtue, Justice, Love, Beauty, or something else? And how do I know if this thing I hold to is truly something worthy of my Ultimate Concern? With these questions in mind, we now turn to the subject of authority; specifically, on what authority do we rely for the truths informing our life? Where do we turn in order to understand the ultimate principles guiding our life, and what type of reason underpins our beliefs?

As I pointed out earlier, both technical and ontological reason hold a valid place in our lives. We cannot (or at least should not) live without either, for they each serve a vital purpose. But sadly, we commonly see two growing groups of people today who fall prey to this false either/or choice: the anti-science religionists on the one hand (fundamentalists), and the anti-religious rationalists/scientists ("atheists") on the other. The religious group cannot accept many basic scientific truths because these truths seemingly threaten the biblical stories on which their religious faith is built. For example, science tells us the world is billions of years older than the 6,000 years fundamentalists hold to; thus, science is a major threat to fundamentalists. On the other hand, the scientific group cannot accept anything religious because they think the only valid form of reason is scientific, technical reason. They relegate anything not scientifically verifiable to mere emotion, thereby completely discounting anything religious.

On both the religious and scientific sides there are people who, quite self-confidently, think they hold the entire truth. Then, there are also people who don't want to take on the task of finding truth for themselves, so they simply follow someone else's truths as their own. Because of these seeming conflicts within reason and knowledge, many people remain unsure as to where to turn for the truth. And this is the crisis of authority. Where in the world should one turn for an authority to validate truth? And what should define truth?

To answer these questions, Tillich points out how conflicts in reason, truth, and authority have led people in one of three general directions: *autonomy*, *heteronomy*, or *theonomy*. Loosely translated, these three words mean—in order—"self law," "strange law," and "divine law." Understanding these three terms will help us better see the roots of the many conflicts we find today between reason and authority, and science and religion.

First, there is autonomy (self-law). *Autonomy means an individual is ultimately obedient to the law of reason found within him or herself.* This would describe, for example, someone who sees scientific or philosophical reason as their ultimate authority. For these people, sound truths can be discovered through science and philosophy because within the self there is a rational structure, a law of logic, if you will, allowing us to know the nature of truth. As such, the individual self is the ultimate authority in verifying the truth. For the autonomously-minded person, there are no transcendent or spiritual truths, only truths discovered in the objective world through scientific or philosophical inquiry. And for Tillich, herein lies the danger with autonomy: in being single-mindedly focused on the objective world, one can cut one's self off from understanding or sensing any transcendent meaning or value in life. In other words, autonomy can lead to a life largely—or sometimes entirely—focused on preliminary, finite concerns. Examples would be people whose primary concern in life is the acquisition of wealth or power, or people who are obsessed with technology or sports. But on the positive side, there are also people who find meaning in their life through scientific or philosophical pursuits.

Second, there is heteronomy ("strange law"). *Quite the opposite of autonomy, heteronomy means an individual, rather than finding ultimate truth within one's self, is obedient to an outside finite religious, social, or political authority claiming to speak in the name of a higher power—such as a church or authoritarian political regime.* As Tillich points out, autonomy often maintains itself simply as a protest against this heteronomous submission to an outside authority. For the autonomous person, there is nothing worse than submitting to someone else's demands or ideologies. Thus, an autonomous person will rightly protest against a religious or political power they feel is taking away their ability to decide, or act, for themselves.

The real danger with heteronomy is that a person surrenders his or her own autonomous reason to an authority above them simply because the authority claims to possess some power or knowledge, whether political, religious, or otherwise. Almost without fail, this authoritarian power will claim to speak in an unconditional and ultimate way. An example of heteronomy in terms of religion would be the Pope's claim of doctrinal infallibility. And on the quasi-religious and political side we see heteronomy exhibited by repressive communist or fascist regimes that claim to speak with some ultimate, unquestioned authority (Hitler and modern-day North Korea are good examples). Both of these heteronomous groups make the individual surrender their own reason to the service of a supposed "higher" reason.

And third, there is theonomy ("divine law"). Before describing this form of authority within reason, it must be emphasized that "divine" here does not mean some supernatural authority that comes from above, or from another realm. What it speaks of is reason in the form of *logos*; an innate principle of reason which orders the cosmos and the human understanding of it. That said, according to Tillich, theonomy is the proper alternative to the narrow stances of both autonomy and heteronomy. *Theonomy is when an individual follows his or her autonomous reason, but this reason is united with its own ultimate, or religious, depth.* In a theonomous situation, one's everyday technical or scientific reason is as solid as ever, but shining through it is a sense of the transcendent meaning of life. In other words, there is an ecstatic element to truth. Reason still serves to explain the everyday material elements of our life—with scientific, political, economic, artistic, or philosophical truths—but it always points to something deeper beneath these truths.

To help better understand theonomy in terms of its moral implications, we need to go back to one of Tillich's most basic ideas covered earlier, namely, that humans are internally split—we have an essential nature and an existential nature. Religion exists because we recognize this split between *what we are (is)* and *what we feel we should be (ought)*. As William James put it, "The man's interior is a battle-ground for what he feels to be two deadly hostile selves, one actual, the other ideal."[45]

This is the essence of morality, and it causes us to strive to reconcile ourselves, to make ourselves whole. And the process of overcoming the estrangement we experience in all dimensions of our lives is aided by a theonomous perspective. Why? Because the very foundation of theonomy is a desire to seek a unity with all of reality.

If we look at morality from the perspective of autonomy, there's a belief that to fully understand life and to know what humans are, or should be, all we need is more technical knowledge about the world and ourselves. In other words, for the autonomously-minded person morality is inherently a technical problem for which we just need more scientific information, e.g., how the mind is structured and how the processes and chemicals in our brain motivate us. On the other hand, with heteronomy the moral perspective is entirely different. Here, we are asked—or sometimes even forced—to follow the rules religious or political groups have set down for us in order to become what we are supposed to be. Morality here is a power, or authority, problem; all we need in order to become who we are supposed to be is the ability, or discipline, to follow the moral dictates of a central religious or political authority. This might include following the Ten Commandments to the letter (Protestantism), the papal doctrines (Catholicism), or the law of Muhammad (Islam).

From the theonomous perspective, both of these options—autonomy and heteronomy—limit the full range of reason's ability to grasp and shape reality in a creative, productive way. For instance, in the case of heteronomy we should not sacrifice our ability to reason simply because some authority tells us they have the truth. And in the case of autonomy we should not rely solely on scientific reason, because it reduces life to technical analysis only, and fails to recognize or express any sense of transcendent meaning behind its material discoveries. For Tillich, a theonomous reason is superior because the culture it creates seeks to communicate something ultimate in all of its creations, whether scientific, political, or artistic.

The Renaissance is one historical period exemplifying a theonomous culture; here, the scientific and philosophical advancements it made were usually grounded in a striving for virtue, truth, and self-transcendence. During this period, theonomous groups, people, or movements tried to let something of ultimate meaning and value shine through them, whether it was a scientific discovery, an artistic creation, or a political or philosophical theory. As such, while firmly grounded in the logic of everyday life, theonomy is also self-transcendent in its spirit; it unites elements from both technical and ontological reason. Theonomy also places a high valuation on individual self-creation, self-critique, and self-expression; for this reason, theonomy stands against any authoritarian power seeking to stifle or eradicate individual self-expression or freedom. And while religious in nature, theonomy always supports valid demands for political, social, and economic justice; scientific integrity; and artistic expression.

Now that we understand the two types of reason, as well as the three different forms of authority humans generally find themselves choosing between, we can see that in the modern world many people have chosen from two narrow worldviews: 1) *autonomy*, a strictly rational perspective that offers a very accurate description of the physical world and its structure and processes, but which usually limits our understanding of the depth of life and what it means to be human, or 2) *heteronomy*, a limited religious understanding of life seeking to answers life's questions, but which requires one to give up individual reason, reject science, and/or accept statements and beliefs which contradict how we know the world works.

Both these worldviews threaten to drive the world into ever-more estrangement and destruction. The autonomous, or secular, vision is usually tied to the belief in endless technological possibility, or quantitative "progress." In its *lack of self-transcendence*, it can overvalue human reason and employ technologies and systems of production that objectify and threaten the well-being of humans and the planetary ecosystems. On the other hand, the heteronomous religious vision presupposes a supernatural realm above the natural world; it often sees this world as cursed, and ultimately looks forward to escaping from it. In its *focus on earthly escape* and a quest for personal salvation in a supernatural realm, it often calls for a turning away from the concerns of this world.

Tillich counters both these limited worldviews by describing a theonomous culture: "In theonomy cognitive reason does not develop authoritatively enforced doctrines, nor does it pursue knowledge for the sake of knowledge; it seeks in everything true an expression of the truth which is of ultimate concern, the truth of being as being. . ."[46] In short, when theonomy is present, the meaning of our being and Being-Itself (God) shines through every cultural, political, social, natural, religious, or artistic creation; every realm of knowledge, and existence itself, is seen as sacred and capable of opening up and revealing the ultimate meaning of existence. Contrary to this, in autonomy no dimension of existence is seen as inherently sacred, and in heteronomy only authoritatively-determined dimensions of existence are seen as sacred.

4

MIRACLES, REVELATION, AND THE EXPERIENCE OF ECSTASY

> *"Revelation is not information about divine things; it is the ecstatic manifestation of the Ground of Being in events, persons, and things. Such manifestations have shaking, transforming, and healing power."*[47]

"Revelation," "miracle," and "resurrection" are words of which many people are rightfully wary. They conjure up images of supernatural events that completely contradict the laws of nature. For Tillich, these supernatural interpretations of the words distort their true religious meanings. As we've seen, Tillich posits that belief in events running counter to natural laws is not faith, but is just belief in magic. And magic does not open us up to the ultimate meaning of our being, which is one of the main elements in the concept of a miracle. So let's start by looking at how Tillich understands this word "miracle."

According to Tillich, a miracle is essentially an "event that produces astonishment." He gives three criteria for a miracle: 1) it is unusual and shocking, but it does not contradict the laws of nature, 2) it points to the mystery of being, and 3) it is received in an ecstatic way. He sums up the importance of these three characteristics of a miracle: "That which does not shake one by its astonishing character has no revelatory power. That which shakes one without pointing to the mystery of being is not miracle but sorcery. That which is not received in ecstasy is a report about the belief in a miracle, not an actual miracle."[48]

Many people root their faith in whether or not Jesus was raised from the dead, or whether he performed miracles. Tillich thinks this is a huge mistake, and it's why he tries to restore the word miracle to its original meaning. No matter what magical, supernatural acts Jesus may have been able to perform (if any at all), the act of performing a miracle does not show us the meaning of life, show us how we should live our lives, or reveal anything about the meaning of Being-Itself (God). Therefore, to root your faith in something as difficult to prove as a supernatural miracle is to root your faith in magic and not a truly transforming, revelatory event.

In addition to this, when you have to defend miraculous acts contradicting the laws of nature, you make your faith an easy target for others to attack on scientific grounds. This is a major problem with literalistic (fundamentalist) interpretations of the Bible, and Tillich makes an important historical point about this. He states that early on in the New Testament—in an effort to impress upon people the seeming miracle of

Christ's saving function—there was an emphasis on supernatural elements in stories of Jesus *instead* of an emphasis on the power in Jesus to overcome existential destruction under the conditions of life. In short, the supposed magical powers of Christ were emphasized over his basic human power of deeply transforming the lives, worldviews, and existences of those who encountered him.

And this leads us to a central message we often encounter in Tillich's writings on Jesus: *the Christ's function is to represent to humanity what God intends humanity to be.* His function was not to perform miracles so that we would worship him as a divine being sent to earth from another realm. This is idolatry, and it's why Tillich claims that the only valid revelation is one which transforms us, but which in the process also negates itself so that it doesn't become yet another object of worship. This is the essence of Jesus' crucifixion, and it's what led Tillich to call Christ's revelation "final," because it "has the power of negating itself without losing itself."[49] We'll cover this topic more in-depth in chapter 8.

For now, we must avoid the temptation to see miracles as supernatural acts performed by Jesus in order to gain special power or recognition. We also must avoid the common mistake of fundamentalism: emphasizing the supernatural elements of Jesus' miracles to the extent that the more absurd or unbelievable a miracle seems, the more religious value it supposedly has. Tillich emphatically mocks this fundamentalist belief: "The more impossible, the more revelatory!"[50] In the end, we have to see that Christ is not some magician who performs miracles in order to be worshipped. As mentioned earlier, Pope Francis recently came out publicly with this very point.

Properly understood, miracles are rare events that have the power to alter the course of human history when individuals and groups are grasped by them on an existential level. The very fact the early Christians seemed so completely astonished by what they saw in Christ's actions—a consistent overcoming of the destructive conflicts of everyday human life—shows the powerful and paradoxical nature of miracles. That's why Tillich says we should see miracles not as magic; rather, we should see them as the transformative power in Jesus to overcome existential destruction and, in the process, point us toward the ground and meaning of our being (God).

One of Tillich's main points about miracles concerns the fact that Jesus was fully human: "Miracles are performed by him [Jesus] because he fully participates in the misery of the human situation and tries to overcome it wherever the occasion offers itself."[51] Whether or not Jesus literally fed the masses with a few fish and loaves of bread, we'll never know—and it's really not important to Tillich. What we do know is that Jesus performed actions that had transforming and healing effects on those who witnessed them. And though Tillich sees Jesus as fully human, this transformative power led to him being called "divine," because in his actions he was transparent to the sacred ground of all being, or God. This does not mean he was a spirit in a man's body sent from a heavenly realm. And the success of Jesus' mission can be seen to this very day, to the extent that his transforming and healing powers lead people to see the ground of being and meaning (God) in themselves and others, and thus overcome the existential destruction in their own lives (guilt, hatred, loneliness, anxiety, anger, intolerance, injustice, aggression).

And now the issue of resurrection. According to Tillich, there are three main theories concerning the resurrection of Jesus: the *physical*, the *spiritualistic*, and the *psychological*. Let me briefly present them, and then lay out Tillich's own theory, which he calls the *restitution theory*.

The physical theory, which Tillich says is the most beautifully expressed of them all, is exactly what it sounds like: the belief that Jesus' body was lifted from the tomb up into heaven. This theory uses physical categories (the presence or absence of a body) to interpret the meaning of resurrection. Tillich sees two problems with this theory. First, "The sources of this story are rather late and questionable, and there is no indication of it in the earliest tradition concerning the event of the Resurrection, namely I Corinthians, chapter 15."[52] And the second problem is that "the absurd question arises as to what happened to the molecules which comprise the corpse of Jesus of Nazareth."[53] In other words, if we follow Tillich's opposition to the supernatural explanations of things, then if Jesus was revived from death, where did his body literally go?

The second theory, the spiritualistic, is largely based on the visions Paul has of Jesus' immaterial spirit, or soul, after his crucifixion. Rather than proof of Jesus' actual resurrection, Tillich claims this theory is simply an attempt to prove the immortality of the soul and its ability to manifest itself to the living after its death. This theory's main problem is that it can't explain the reappearance of Jesus' total personality, including his bodily presence.[54] It also relies on the supernatural belief in the existence of "spirits," something Tillich is continually out to debunk.

The third theory, the psychological, Tillich describes as "an inner event in the minds of Jesus' adherents." He points out that this theory "does not imply that the event was 'merely' psychological, namely, dependent on psychological factors in the minds of those who Paul enumerates (e.g., an intensification of the memory of Jesus). However, the psychological theory misses the reality of the event which is presupposed in the symbol—the event of the Resurrection of the Christ."[55]

Tillich sees each of these three theories as flawed, so he offers his own theory of what resurrection means. His "restitution theory" states: "In an ecstatic experience the concrete picture of Jesus of Nazareth became indissolubly united with the reality of the New Being. He is present wherever the New Being is present. Death was not able to push him into the past."[56] For Tillich, Jesus' resurrected presence is something more than physical, psychological, or supernatural explanations can reach. And this is why he says Christ's resurrected presence "does not have the character of a revived (and transmuted body), nor does it have the character of a reappearance of an individual soul; it has the character of spiritual presence. . . This event happened first to some of his followers who had fled to Galilee in the hours of his execution; then to many others; then to Paul; then to all those who in every period experience his living presence here and now."[57] In other words, Jesus' being and presence was such a transformative and ecstatic experience for his disciples that it left an indelible mark on them; he lived on "resurrected" in the fabric and memory of their being. And this radical experience, this new reality that Christ brought about, is the basis for Tillich's description of him as the "New Being."

Standing against the old state of things in human life—a state characterized by existential estrangement—the New Being is one "in which the self-estrangement of our existence is overcome, a reality of reconciliation and reunion, or creativity, meaning, and hope."[58] This is why, for Tillich, "resurrection" is existential, because it concerns every dimension of our existence. And this new state of things is not something that happened only when Christ was alive, or when he was crucified. It happened then, it happens now, and it will happen in every future moment that the resurrected power of Christ's being manifests in acts of human love or forgiveness, or every time existential self-destruction and estrangement is overcome in human life.

Resurrection, then, is not an event in the past; resurrection is the ongoing power of the New Being to create healing and love now. So rather than the idea that resurrection is an event that *happened*, Tillich says resurrection is something that *happens*: "Resurrection happens now, or it does not happen at all. It happens in and around us, in soul and history, in nature and universe."[59] As you can see from this quote, resurrection also has implications for the entire universe, not just for humans. I will cover this idea in more detail later but, for now, we need to address another religious word that has become distorted, namely, "revelation."

As shown in the opening quote to this chapter, a true revelation (or revelatory event) brings about a state of consciousness where the depth of life's structure and meaning (God) shines through everything we experience. A revelation does this because it is a shocking or mysterious event; it grasps us and opens us up to another dimension of experience we had not previously known. A true revelatory event shows us what should concern us ultimately by revealing the depth of reality—the "really real," as Tillich puts it—behind the transitoriness of everything else around us. And, I would contend, when all of reality is imbued with this sense of ultimacy, then we act accordingly by showing deep respect to others, the natural world, and ourselves; in other words, we act as Jesus did.

Like miracles, revelation is paradoxical because our everyday understanding of reality is shaken or transformed; we are placed in a situation of accepting something that exists beyond our common understanding. Unfortunately, many people think this means reason must be set aside in order to accept the possibility of things existing in ways other than we usually understand them. And this takes us back to our earlier discussion about the two types of reason, technical/scientific vs. ontological. When confronted by something miraculous or revelatory, our common reason is not thrown out, but it is transcended. A revelatory experience preserves reason, but goes beyond it. This is why Tillich calls ontological reason the "depth of reason"; it brings us into contact with deep experiences and ideas that we have come to call "religious." Admittedly, many people have never had these experiences because they've never opened themselves up for the possibility of them. Or they've had these experiences, but are afraid to call them "religious" because of the negative connotations associated with the word.

As I pointed out earlier, the term Tillich uses to describe revelatory or miraculous experiences is "ecstasy," and it's worth quoting him at length on the meaning of the term:

> 'Ecstasy' ("standing outside of one's self") points to a state of mind which is extraordinary in the sense that the mind transcends its ordinary situation. Ecstasy is not the negation of reason; it is the state of mind in which reason is beyond itself, that is, beyond its subject-object structure. In being beyond itself reason does not deny itself. 'Ecstatic reason' remains reason; it does not receive anything irrational or antirational—which it could not do without self-destruction—but it transcends the basic condition of finite rationality, the subject-object structure. This is the state mystics try to reach by ascetic and meditative activities. . . Ecstasy occurs only if the mind is grasped by the mystery, namely, the ground of being and meaning. And, conversely, there is no revelation without ecstasy. At best there is information which can be tested scientifically.[60]

Because Tillich believes all dimensions of our life have the potential for opening us up to the meaning of our being and Being-Itself (God), an ecstatic or revelatory experience can come through music, art, the love of another person, or through communion with nature—to name a few. This latter experience is why he often speaks of sacredness in the natural world, as well as why nature shares in the ultimate fate of humanity.[61] The experience Tillich ultimately describes with the term ecstasy is one we've all had before. Often coming as a sudden upwelling of emotion, it can cause a mild shortness of breath, a flush of inner warmth, a feeling of complete acceptance and humility, and quite frequently, tears. It is often accompanied by the feeling of being at one with all of Being, and/or all beings.

Tillich's understanding of ecstasy is what causes him to speak affirmatively of mystics and the meditative state, as well as how the idea of a "saint" exemplifies this experience. Unfortunately, the term saint has come to mean someone who is morally or religiously perfect. But according to Tillich, "sainthood is not personal perfection. Saints are persons who are transparent for the ground of being which is revealed through them. . . "[62] In other words, though they are merely human, some people are able to reveal the sacred by living an ecstatic life—a life not characterized by existential estrangement but, rather, one exhibiting radical love.

After covering some of the basic concepts of Christianity and how Tillich sees their distortion affecting modern religion, it's now time to go back to something covered early on in the book, namely, his "method of correlation." Tillich's basic premise is that when we analyze the human situation and its accompanying problems with the aid of psychology and philosophy—specifically, existentialism—we find that the symbols of Christianity provide the answers, or solutions, to those problems.

5

EXISTENTIALISM, THE SPIRITUAL PRESENCE, AND THE CONQUEST OF RELIGION

"In the depth of every living religion there is a point at which the religion itself loses its importance, and that to which it points breaks through its particularity, elevating it to spiritual freedom and with it to a vision of the spiritual presence in other expressions of the ultimate meaning of man's existence."[63]

One of the defining characteristics of humans—differentiating us from all other beings—is our acute awareness of our existence. Other animals are primarily, though obviously not entirely, bound to act out of a stimulus and response mechanism to the conditions in their immediate environment. Humans, on the other hand, have the power (and responsibility) of choosing to act in one way or another. This is what allows us, to a certain degree, to create our destinies. This freedom—in fact, necessity—of choosing to become what we want is a gift that gives humanity its greatness.

But this freedom can also become a curse. There are several reasons for this: we can fail to make the correct choices and contradict our own intentions; our choices can come into conflict with other peoples' choices and we can do harm to them; we can make choices that objectify or exploit other humans or other species; we can become desperately overwhelmed by the multitude of choices facing us and experience deep loneliness, guilt, emptiness, or meaninglessness; or we can reach a state of disease or desperation and wish life would end so that we wouldn't have to face making any more choices at all. As Tillich sees it, all these possibilities bring us face to face with the moral act. And failing to act as we should—that is, failure to actualize our true, or essential, self—is the essence of the moral problem.

This moral problem is at the heart of the philosophy of existentialism, for existentialism is concerned with understanding human nature and the internal and external challenges that accompany our existence. Though Tillich and many other existentialists believe humans are composed of two basic dimensions—an *essential* nature and an *existential* nature—some existentialist philosophers, perhaps most notably, Jean-Paul Sartre, denied this distinction, arguing that it's impossible to speak of a "human nature" at all.

According to Sartre, because humans have complete freedom there is no inherent, static nature that can be ascribed to us at all. But Tillich pointed out the logical absurdity of

Sartre's argument by turning it on its head: if humans have *complete freedom*—as opposed to the biological necessity of other beings—isn't that very characteristic, freedom, the basis of our human nature? Of all beings on the earth, only humans have complete conscious freedom to question and go beyond the givenness of our existence.

To Tillich, this uniquely human characteristic leads to moral problems because, as he sees it, our essential nature is how God (the Ground of our being) intends us to be, while our existential nature is how we actually are. This creates an internal moral struggle within us, which causes us to strive for what we sense we "ought" to be. And this is why all religions are in agreement that the state of human existence is the state of estrangement. Tillich boils it down quite succinctly: "The state of existence is the state of estrangement. Man is estranged from the ground of his being (God), from other beings, and from himself."[64] He goes further by clarifying the complexity of our moral existence: "Man as he exists is not what he essentially is and ought to be. He is estranged from his true being. The profundity of the term 'estrangement' lies in the implication that one belongs essentially to that from which one is estranged. Man is not a stranger to his true being, for he belongs to it."[65] Religion, then, is the collective drive of humans to overcome the estrangement, guilt, anxiety, and meaninglessness we face when making difficult moral choices. In the company of others seeking to bring about their essential selves, religion serves (or at least should serve) as the primary support in these efforts.

The estrangement of which Tillich speaks can manifest itself in many ways. Let me give just two examples, one personal and one social. On the personal side, estrangement manifests when unconscious forces within us, or conscious bad choices, cause us to do things we know are not true to our essential nature. This can manifest in negative emotions such as guilt, emptiness, or sadness, to name a few. On the social side, estrangement can manifest in the political, economic, gender, religious, or cultural domination, leading to exploitation and/or harm to a particular group.

This is why, for Tillich, existentialism is largely a philosophy of revolt. For instance, accompanying the rise of industrialization and worldwide capitalist expansion, humans have found themselves increasingly dehumanized in order to fit into this massive and fast-paced method of production and mode of existence. Existentialism confronts this forced estrangement by pointing out the ways humanity's authentic existence is distorted under these unnecessary, man-made conditions (e.g., Marxist theory). And Tillich connects this existentialist revolt with the practical and essential message of Christianity:

> The problem of an economic system able to give security of permanent full employment and certainty of decent livelihood for all lies much more largely in the realms of political and moral decisions. It is in the realms in which religious principles are decisive. Christianity can insist that the virtually infinite productive capacities of mankind shall be used for

> the advantage of everyone, instead of being restricted and wasted by the profit interests of a controlling class and the struggle for power between different groups within that class. Christianity should reveal and destroy the vicious circle of production of means and ends, which in turn become means without any ultimate end. It must liberate man from bondage to an incalculable and inhuman system of production that absorbs the creative powers of his soul by ruthless competition, fear, despair, and the utter sense of meaninglessness. . . Christianity must support plans for economic reorganization that promise to overcome the antithesis of absolutism and individualism, even if such plans imply a revolutionary transformation of the present social structure and the liquidation of large vested interests.[66]

Here, Tillich points out the necessity of applying the Christian message to basic economic and political realities. Modern fundamentalists, by and large, refuse to do this because it would upset the interests of the moneyed, capitalist class they now largely serve. This hypocritical attitude of Christians who refuse to fairly allocate the world's bounty to provide all humans with a basic level of material existence, forms the basis for Tillich's rather incendiary statement on revolutions: "The principal antirevolutionary attitude of many Christian groups is fundamentally wrong, whether unbloody cultural or unbloody and bloody political revolutions are concerned. The chaos which follows any kind of revolution can be a creative chaos."[67] Just as he believes there are just wars—World War II being a prime example—Tillich also believes that political and economic revolutions are sometimes justified. If a dominant class or group is physically or economically oppressing another group, then it's justified to aggressively oppose this group in the name of Christian justice for all.

To sum up, social estrangement occurs when one group exerts its power over another group (cultural, religious, economic, or political estrangement), and personal estrangement can arise internally when forces cause us to rebel against ourselves and our own best interests (inner, or psychological, estrangement). Forms of personal estrangement can be addressed in many cases with philosophical counseling or psychotherapy, and Tillich often pointed out how depth psychology is effective in alleviating feelings such as guilt, anxiety, or meaninglessness. That said, he also believes psychotherapy can only go so far, for "the state of existence is the state of estrangement." In other words, the negative forces in life that keep us from perfect relations with others and ourselves exist simply as a part of the nature of being. We can address it with psychotherapy, but these efforts will only go so deep.

Similarly, the social estrangement we see in economic, political, or cultural situations can often be addressed through the restructuring of society. The idea is that if we just change the way we relate to ourselves and the world, then such existential estrangement and the many negative forces in society causing such estrangement—what Tillich calls "structures of destruction"—will disappear. Throughout history, the radical line of this type of thinking has been called *utopianism*. What utopianism fails to see, however, is that estrangement exists not just because of how we structure society (communist or capitalist or tribal); it happens because estrangement is in the very fabric of human existence itself. You can change the structure of society in as many positive directions as possible—and this should be the goal of our collective social and moral development—but one thing that will not disappear is the inherent estranged nature of human existence, manifested in guilt, anxiety, meaninglessness, fear of death, emptiness, and doubt. This, of course, is only a list of the negative characteristics humans experience—the list of positives easily equals it.

With this brief survey of existentialism and morality in mind, one might assume that Tillich sees religion as holding the key to life's ultimate problems. In fact, his following quote may seem to imply just that: "Existentialism is an analysis of the human predicament. And the answers to the questions implied in man's predicament are religious, whether open or hidden."[68] But the case isn't so clear-cut, as we see in the opening quote to this chapter. Rather than pointing to religion as the answer, Tillich wants to show that, as a finite human endeavor itself, religion also falls prey to the estranging, destructive elements characterizing life:

> Since religion is the self-transcendence of life in the realm of the spirit, it is in religion that man starts the quest for unambiguous life and it is in religion that he receives the answer. But

> the answer is not identical with religion, since religion itself is ambiguous. The fulfillment of the quest for unambiguous life transcends any religious form or symbol in which it is expressed.[69]

These words sum up why Tillich often speaks of the distinction between religion in the *narrow* sense of the word versus religion in the *universal* sense. In the universal sense, Tillich says everyone is religious by virtue of being human and having to face the deep questions concerning the meaning of life. In the narrow sense of the word, only certain people follow religious teachings and doctrines—and, as we know, these teachings are often quite divergent from each other. The common core of all religion, however, is the honest quest to understand what we're supposed to be (our essential self), and then actualize that through the moral act—however ambiguously or fragmentarily.

One could assume that moral actualization would take place most readily in the churches. But this is not always the case. Tillich is very blunt: "The churches rarely followed the attitude of Jesus toward the 'publicans and whores.' They were and are ashamed of the way in which Jesus acted in acknowledging the equality of all men under sin (which they confess) and therefore the equality of all men under forgiveness (which they confess)."[70] We could, of course, give a long list of other ways in which the Christian Church fails to live up to, or even contradicts, the message of Jesus. Not only do we find copious examples of estrangement and moral contradictions within the churches, sometimes they are even more evident there.

Speaking as a Protestant minister himself, Tillich expresses this problem well when he speaks of the weakness of the Catholic doctrine of papal infallibility: "The fact that the Roman church does not acknowledge the ambiguity of its own papal leadership saves it from the obvious ambiguities of leadership but gives it a demonic quality. The Protestant weakness of continuous self-criticism is its greatness and a symptom of the Spiritual impact upon it."[71] For Tillich, the Catholic belief that a fallible human being—the Pope—can somehow possess infallible truth is a form of hubris and religious idolatry. He even goes so far as to call it "demonic"—meaning the act of someone claiming to speak from divine authority when one is, in fact, only finite and human.

When Tillich speaks above of the "Protestant weakness of continuous self-criticism," he is actually referring to the strength of one of its main elements: the "Protestant Principle." This term simply means there is, or at least should be, a constant effort in Protestantism to avoid making itself and its teachings absolute: "The Protestant Principle is an expression of the conquest of religion by the Spiritual Presence and consequently an expression of the victory over the ambiguities of religion, its profanization, and its demonization. It is Protestant because it protests against the tragic-demonic self-elevation of religion and liberates religion from itself. . ."[72] In simpler terms, Protestantism's continual self-criticism keeps it from making the idolatrous claim that it has the only avenue to religious truth.

Protestantism might claim to be witness to the truth of Jesus as the Christ—and the effect of the healing power of this truth on the lives of its members—but it does not, or at least should not, claim to express this truth perfectly in its actions. And this self-criticism is at the root of its concept of "the priesthood of all believers"—the idea that no religious authority is ultimately necessary to mediate a relationship between an individual believer and God. This is the opposite of Catholicism, which is based on a hierarchical structure with the priest above the congregation members in all matters; there is no access to God except through the Catholic Church.

While Protestantism is rooted in a continual questioning, and even doubt, about its ability to adequately express the Christian message, Catholicism is rooted in its absolute certainty in the expression of this message. In its lack of questioning and doubt Tillich sees a major danger—whether in Catholicism or in any other religion prone to fanaticism. He uses the mission of Jesus to illustrate this point:

> Those who are not able to elevate their doubts into the truth which transcends every finite truth must repress them. They perforce become fanatical. Yet no traces of fanaticism are present in the biblical picture. Jesus does not claim absolute certitude. . . He rejects the fanatical attitude of the disciples who do not follow him. In the power of certitude . . . he accepts incertitude as an element of finiteness.[73]

What Tillich emphasizes here is that humans have always been plagued by deep feelings of doubt, including Jesus himself.

How we deal with this inescapable human reality is the important thing; there are healthy ways and unhealthy ways. When fundamentalist adherents of any religion fail to recognize the importance of this point they become fanatical, prideful, or even violent towards others with conflicting views. All of these are inherently anti-religious characteristics, and all show how fundamentalist fanaticism distorts the true, healthy meaning of religion.

Unlike most theologians, Tillich was quite comfortable speaking of the healthy nature of doubt, particularly for those whom the institutionalized religions no longer spoke. And this is why he spoke famously of the "God Above God." In this concept he expresses the universal nature of faith, saying that sometimes in doubt

> the God of both religious and theological language disappears. But something remains, namely, the seriousness of that doubt in which meaning within meaninglessness is affirmed. The source of this affirmation of meaning within meaninglessness, of certitude within doubt, is not the God of traditional theism but the 'God above God,' the power of being, which works through those who have no name for it, not even the name God.[74]

To the Christian fundamentalist, who believes the only way to salvation is by becoming a Christian and being "born again," such a statement would seem entirely heretical, perhaps even anti-Christian. But Tillich would disagree. In an interview late in his life, Tillich said he had numerous encounters with non-religious people throughout his life through whom he felt the love of Jesus working, even though they might not have known—or perhaps even rejected—any ultimate significance of Jesus.

When Tillich speaks above of a power "which works through those who have no name for it" he is referring to one of his key concepts: the "Spiritual Presence." He defines it as a "divine presence in creaturely life." But before we mistake what he means by this, let's remember that, much like God or gravity or love, "the Spiritual Presence" is a reality one can know of through experience, but it is not an object that "exists." So to counter common supernatural ideas about the existence of spirits that inhabit human bodies or the heavens, Tillich uses some biblical references to explain this power in the following non-supernatural way:

> The Spiritual Presence is not an intoxicating substance, or a stimulus for psychological excitement, or a miraculous physical cause. It cannot cause . . . the removal of a person from one place to another 'through the air'. . . the generation of an embryo in the mother's womb without male participation, or the knowledge of foreign languages without a process of learning. All these effects are considered as caused by the Spiritual Presence. Obviously, if these stories are taken literally, they make the divine

Spirit a finite, though extraordinary, cause beside other causes. In this view Spirit is a kind of physical matter.[75]

In this one paragraph, Tillich debunks several biblical stories that millions of people have interpreted as supernatural miracles caused by a spiritual being. At the same time, we saw him opening up the idea that the Spiritual Presence is potentially present in all humans, whether religious or not. This appears when he talks of a wider definition of religion, with every human having an unconditional concern, or faith, concerning some ultimate principle—whether consciously acknowledged or not.

By expanding the concept of religion through the Spiritual Presence, Tillich's wider definition guards against those within the church who claim a special relationship with the divine, and who then use this supposed special relationship to wield power or judgment over others. As Tillich states, "The Spiritual Presence excludes fanaticism, because in the presence of God no man can boast about his grasp of God. No one can grasp that by which he is grasped—the Spiritual Presence."[76] In short, humans cannot claim to possess either the ultimate truth, or the reality they worship; properly understood, they are witness to both and are possessed by both.

The Spiritual Presence, by definition, should lead to humility, the increased union of people with one another, and the overcoming of estrangement—not the distancing and separation of one person from another. This is why fanaticism in religion is a distorting, demonic force revealing the presence of negativities inherent in religion itself. In the end, fanaticism destroys the human spirit by cutting off the Spiritual Presence. And without the Spiritual Presence, the real self-transcendence needed to overcome estrangement remains hidden or distorted.

As we continually see, Tillich explains reality in non-supernatural terms. In other words, he opposes the existence of physical or even immaterial "spirits," or any other special forces, causing things to happen that undercut the natural laws governing the universe. So instead of seeing life cut up into two levels, the physical (natural) and the meta-physical (supernatural), he defines life as a collection of overlapping dimensions; these dimensions are *always* unified in one coherent universe. In ascending order, the dimensions are: the inorganic, organic, biological, psychological, historical, and spiritual. We'll delve deeper into this interesting classification of Tillich's in Chapter 7 when discussing his concept of the "multidimensional unity of life." For now, it's important to focus on the spirit dimension, and how it relates to the Spiritual Presence in humans.

Because we are limited in our ability to communicate with other advanced nonhuman animal species, we must say for now that the spiritual dimension is, as far as we know, only outwardly manifest in human life. Other species may embody the inorganic, organic, biological, and even psychological dimensions, but only humanity embodies the dimensions of history and spirit—the latter Tillich defines as "the union of power and meaning." But again, the spirit dimension is not a thing that exists; it is a dimension of consciousness and meaningful intention that makes humans human. Tillich provides us with a precise and beautiful description of how the human dimension of spirit can be grasped by the Spiritual Presence:

> The spirit, a dimension of finite life, is driven into a successful self-transcendence; it is grasped by something ultimate and unconditional. It is still the human spirit; it remains what it is, but at the same time, it goes out of itself under the impact of the divine Spirit. 'Ecstasy' is the classical term for this state of being grasped by the Spiritual Presence. It describes the human situation under the Spiritual Presence exactly.
>
> Although the ecstatic character of the experience of Spiritual Presence does not destroy the rational structure of the human spirit it does something the human spirit could not do by itself. When it grasps man, it creates unambiguous life. Man in his self-transcendence can reach for it, but man cannot grasp it, unless he is first grasped by it.[77]

With this brief discussion of the Spiritual Presence we can see that, for Tillich, the purpose of religion has much less to do with believing in church dogma than it does with opening oneself up to a life of self-transcendent meaning. This process of finding Spiritual maturity is what he terms "sanctification," and for Tillich there are four main characteristics of a mature life lived under the Spiritual Presence: increasing awareness; increasing freedom; increasing relatedness; and increasing transcendence.[78] Taking each one of these individually, Tillich explains how a life of spiritual maturity will exhibit signs of the Spiritual Presence's impact on it.

Tillich says the first principle, *increased awareness*, is

> the principle according to which man in the process of sanctification becomes increasingly aware of his actual situation and of the forces struggling around him and his humanity but also becomes aware of the answers to the questions implied in this situation. . . Such awareness. . . does not lead to the Stoic 'wise man,' who is superior to the ambiguities of life because he has conquered his passions and desires, but rather an awareness of these ambiguities in himself, as in everyone, and to the power of affirming life and its vital dynamics in spite of its ambiguities. Such awareness includes sensitivity toward the demands of one's own growth, toward the hidden hopes and disappointments within others, toward the voiceless voice of a concrete situation, toward the grades of authenticity in the life of the spirit in others and oneself.[79]

The Spiritual Presence's impact on human spiritual maturity also shows itself in the second principle, *increased freedom*:

> The more one is reunited with his true being under the impact of the Spirit, the more one is free from the commandments of the law. . . In so far as we are estranged, prohibitions and commandments appear and produce an uneasy conscience. In so far as we are reunited, we actualize what we essentially are in freedom, without command.[80]

In other words, the more one is in contact with one's essential self—i.e., the less one is estranged from oneself, others, nature, and God—the less one has to worry about following commandments, because one's natural inclination is already to live as one should. In today's evangelical fundamentalism we find the exact opposite: a heavy emphasis on avoiding certain acts because they are "sinful," as well as commandments to follow other acts because they are "pure." This need to follow commandments and laws points to a lack of being under the impact of the Spiritual Presence. Why? Because when one feels compelled to follow commandments one does not live freely as one's essential self, but rather acts out of fear of what one's existential self might do. The common guilt feelings and the constant need to follow laws of prohibition show the decreased sense of freedom many fundamentalist adherents feel. In the end, no matter how many laws and commandments one may follow perfectly, the result is often a lower level of spiritual freedom—a key component of spiritual maturity.

As for the third principle, *increased relatedness*, Tillich says that "Relatedness implies the awareness of the other one and the freedom to relate to him by overcoming self-seclusion within oneself and within the other one."[81] In short, spiritual maturity will be evidenced in someone's ability to transcend, or reach out, from the depths of one's self and make authentic contact with the another person. Speaking more precisely of the impact of the Spiritual Presence in terms of relatedness, he says:

> There is no way of overcoming self-seclusion lastingly other than the impact of the power which elevates the individual person above himself ecstatically and enables him to find the other person—if the other person is also ready to be elevated above himself. . . Sanctification, or the process toward Spiritual maturity, conquers loneliness by providing for solitude and communion in interdependence. A decisive symptom of Spiritual maturity is the power to sustain solitude.[82]

So these are Tillich's first three principles of a life lived under the impact of the Spiritual Presence: increased awareness, increased freedom, and increased relatedness. What he emphasizes next is that none of these principles—and thus sanctification itself— would be possible without the existence of the fourth principle: *increased transcendence*. For this reason, the principle of transcendence undergirds all the others: "sanctification is not possible without a continuous transcendence of oneself in the direction of the ultimate."[83]

As a short aside, for Tillich the term "holy" means the quality and ability of something, or someone, to point to or express the Ultimate in life. And contrary to the fundamentalist view, "holiness" may be found in objects and people both within and outside of religion. This is why Tillich does not insist that religion, as a particular function of life, is absolutely essential to one's spiritual maturity. In fact, often the opposite is the case. As already discussed, religion is just as susceptible to distortions as any other function of life, be they politics, economics, or other cultural functions. For Tillich, what's important is one's desire and efforts to reach for a deeper relationship with the ground of reality—the Ultimate, or God—whether within the confines of religion, or outside of it altogether:

> In the mature life, determined by the Spiritual Presence, participation in the devotional life of the congregation may be restricted or refused, prayer may be subordinated to meditation, religion in the narrower sense of the word may be denied in the name of religion in the larger sense of the word. . . it may even happen that an increased experience of transcendence leads to an increase in criticism of religion as a special function. But in spite of these qualifying statements,

'self-transcendence' is identical with the attitude of devotion toward that which is ultimate.[84]

In summation of these four principles, we can see that the spiritually mature person will be comfortable with, and find peace in, solitude; she will seek out authentic relations with others and the world; she will have the ability to transcend her own ego in an effort to reach authenticity both within herself and with others; she will have the freedom to act creatively and without the constraint of laws and prohibitions; and she will do all this while sensing the importance of one's inner needs and desire to create meaningful relationships. Tillich sums it up: "The process of sanctification runs toward a state in which the 'search for identity' reaches its goal, which is the identity of the essential self shining through the contingencies of the existing self."[85] In other words, spiritual maturity is present in every act or effort seeking to overcome existential estrangement, and thus create union with all of reality through acts of love.

Tillich wants us to see that spiritual maturity is not limited to only those people who call themselves "religious." Many people consciously remain outside of religion proper, and many others follow different faiths. But, in Tillich's view, this does not mean the Spiritual Presence is not at work in their lives. He expresses this in his understanding of faith as a universal human tendency: "Faith as the state of being opened by the Spiritual Presence to the transcendent unity of unambiguous life is a description which is universally valid despite its particular, Christian background."[86]

This universal definition of faith radically alters the way we should view religion, and it should enable us to see the work of the "spirit" in people who consciously stand outside the churches:

> There are youth alliances, friendship groups, educational, artistic, and political movements, and, even more obviously, individuals without any visible relation to each other in whom the Spiritual Presence's impact is felt, although they are indifferent or hostile to all overt expressions of religion. They do not belong to a church, but they are not excluded from the Spiritual Community. It is impossible to deny this if one looks at the manifold instances of profanization and demonization of the Spiritual Presence in these groups—the churches—which claim to be the Spiritual Community.[87]

Clearly, Tillich has no problem pointing out the hypocrisies and distortions found in the Christian churches. This might seem strange since he himself was a minister and theologian, but the truth of his statements cannot be denied. He even went so far as to say that "If the churches do not feel the call to conversion... they will become obsolete, and the divine Spirit will work in and through seemingly atheistic and anti-Christian movements."[88] This is a pretty challenging statement coming from a Christian. But Tillich expressed these sentiments strongly and consistently throughout his life. And this is why his definitions of faith, the Spiritual Community, and religion are vastly more encompassing than those found in most modern-day expressions of Christianity.

In essence, Tillich wanted to critique all elements of existence and point us toward the depth of life. So while he pointed out many distortions within the church, he also criticized secular society's increasing lack of depth. He did this by decrying the plague of modern mass conformity and the increasing dehumanization spawned by wide-scale industrial production. In all this, he tried to break down boundaries —political, artistic, economic, cultural, and scientific. But the boundary he seemed most concerned with bridging was that of the sacred (religious) and secular (non-religious). He termed this process the "conquest of religion":

> Conquest of religion does not mean secularization but rather the closing of the gap between the religious and the secular by removing both through the Spiritual Presence. This is the meaning of faith as the state of being grasped by that which concerns us ultimately and not as a set of beliefs, even if the object of belief is a divine being. This is the meaning of love as reunion of the separated in all dimensions...[89]

What Tillich envisioned was a society in which there was no concept of the secular, because in a spiritually mature society every act and cultural expression would open up the depth and sacredness of existence. If we were to imagine such a society it would look much like what Tillich describes as a theonomous culture, or the "Spiritual Community." This community, while not necessarily made up of individuals belonging to a Christian Church, would consist of five primary characteristics: it would be ecstatic; it would have certainty of faith, or express the Ultimate in all its actions; it would have self-surrendering love; it would strive for "the ultimate reunion of all the estranged members of mankind"; and it would be open to all individuals, groups, and things.[90] In short, it would express Jesus' being and message.

To get to such a point, Tillich knew there was only one force with the power to move us toward the dissolution of dividing boundaries and estrangement in all its forms. He called this the "drive toward the reunion of the separated,"[91] or love. Love, more than any other reality, has the power to overcome all dimensions of estrangement: within ourselves, between ourselves and others, between ourselves and nature, and between ourselves and God (Being-itself). But Tillich is quick to point out that love is more than just an emotion; it is a fundamental force in the universe: ". . . love is not only related to emotion; it is the whole being's movement toward another being to overcome existential separation."[92]

For Tillich, love is defined by its power to overcome estrangement in all its forms. And he points out the existence of four specific forms of love, each with its varying dynamics of attraction: *libido, philia, eros,* and *agape. Libido* is "the movement of the needy toward that which fulfills the need," *philia* is "the movement of the equal toward union with the equal," and *eros* is "the movement of that which is lower in power and meaning toward to that which is higher."[93] The final form of love, *agape*—typically associated with "Christian love"—is the one Tillich ultimately references when he speaks of overcoming estrangement by the "reunion of the separated." The three previous forms of love are all dependent on the changing conditions of either the lover or the loved, but *agape* transcends all these other forms in power because it is not

> dependent on repulsion and attraction, on passion and sympathy... It affirms the other unconditionally, that is, apart from higher or lower, pleasant or unpleasant qualities. *Agape* unites the lover and the beloved because of the image of fulfillment which God has of both. Therefore, *agape* is universal; no one with whom a concrete relation is technically possible ("the neighbor") is excluded; nor is anyone preferred. *Agape* accepts the other in spite of resistance. It suffers and forgives. It seeks the personal fulfillment of the other.[94]

In essence, *agape* is the form of love we often refer to as "unconditional" because it accepts all people—even the ones who reject us. And it is because of *agape* that Tillich rejects defining love as a strictly emotional phenomenon. When one is grasped by the power of *agape* and seeks the ultimate fulfillment in the other person simply because of their humanity, Tillich believes it's possible to speak symbolically of God, or Being-itself, as love:

> It is false to define love by its emotional side. This leads necessarily to sentimental interpretations of the meaning of love and calls into question its symbolic application to the divine life. But God is love. And, since God is being-itself, one must say that being-itself is love.[95]

Both God and love are *symbols* of realities we experience as humans and, therefore, should not be seen as things. So Tillich's quote about God, or Being-Itself, being love can be summed up quite simply: the Ground of Being (God)—as the basis and reality upholding everything in existence—seeks to express itself to the world through humanity's acts of love. This is a love that includes love of ourselves, love of others, love of nature, and ultimately love of God.

Now if Tillich is correct that love is the drive toward the reunion of the separated in all dimensions of existence, then what is the force that works against love and threatens existence relentlessly with estrangement? To answer this question, we now turn to our next topics: sin and evil.

6

SIN AND EVIL

"It is not the disobedience to a law which makes an act sinful, but the fact that it is an expression of man's estrangement from God, from men, from himself."[96]

As we've now seen, a basic theme running throughout Tillich's writing is that various forms of estrangement keep humans from actualizing their essential, or true, natures. As we've also seen, Tillich characterizes the very nature of existence as estranged. In other words, there is an inherent element of existence that is marked by separation and destruction in all dimensions of life—in bodily life this is called *disease*, in science it's called *entropy*, in politics it's called *revolution*, and in our moral life it is often called *sin*. Tillich wrote about each of these dimensions, but here we're concerned with the latter—morality and the concept of sin. For Tillich, morality is defined by our efforts to actualize our essential self and become whole. How? By overcoming estrangement, however fragmentarily or ambiguously, through acts of love. And one of the primary barriers to such reunion in existence is the presence of sin. But what exactly is sin?

Characteristic of Tillich's uniquely existentialist perspective, the opening quote shows his widened understanding of the concept of sin as "estrangement from God," or from the Ground of one's being. For the fundamentalist Christian, on the other hand, sin can be boiled down very simply to an individual act that is banned by the law of God in the Bible. The problem with such fundamentalist interpretation is that we live in a different time and historical reality than existed in biblical times, and it's exceedingly difficult to apply these ancient events and contexts to the world in which we now live. Because of this, there seems to be many different interpretations nowadays as to what is or is not actually a "sin." Abortion and homosexuality are two examples we see people struggling with today, and there is no clear answer because these issues are barely, if at all, mentioned in the Bible. Jesus certainly never mentions anything about either of them.

For these, and other, reasons Tillich defines sin in a way different than most people have probably understood it: "Sin is a matter of our relation to God and not to ecclesiastical, moral, or social authorities."[97] And this relationship to God, or the Ground of our Being, is composed either of varying degrees of reunion or separation. The problem is that sin today is most commonly seen as personal deviation from moral laws. This definition does not emphasize sin as being the state of estrangement from that to which one belongs—God, one's self, and one's world. And when we focus on sin as an individual personal act that violates some biblical or human law, then we fail to see the larger picture Tillich wants us to see.

Regardless of the term's common misuse, Tillich points to the general usefulness of the concept of sin: "Nevertheless, the word 'sin' cannot be overlooked. It expresses what is not implied in the term 'estrangement,' namely the personal act of turning away from that to which one belongs. Sin expresses most sharply the personal character of estrangement . . . It expresses personal freedom and guilt."[98] So while Tillich sees the word sin misused in ways much like the word faith, he still sees some validity in its usage. And he sees sin composed of three basic elements: unbelief, *hubris*, and concupiscence.

Speaking of the first, Tillich states that "'Unbelief' . . . means the act or state in which man in the totality of his being turns away from God. In his existential self-realization he turns toward himself and his world and loses his essential unity with the ground of his being and his world."[99] The second element of sin, *hubris*, is commonly exemplified in the stories of Greek tragedies, and Tillich sees it as the core element of sin. Commonly interpreted as "pride," he expresses it this way: "In estrangement, man is outside the divine center to which his own center essentially belongs. He is the center of himself and his world."[100] He then goes on to speak of both the value *and* danger in this centeredness, which

> gives man his greatness, dignity, and being, in the 'image of God.' It indicates his ability to transcend both himself and his world, to look

> at both, and to see himself in perspective as the center in which all parts of his world converge. To be a self and to have a world constitute the challenge to man as the perfection of creation.
>
> But this perfection is, at the same time, his temptation. Man is tempted to make himself existentially the center of himself and his world.[101]

In other words, we are tempted to make of ourselves more than we are, elevating ourselves to a level beyond our own limited finitude, failing to face the fact that we are, in fact, finite. This definition of *hubris* echoes Tillich's earlier definition of idolatry as the elevation of something finite and transitory into something of seemingly ultimate value. It also underscores why he saw *hubris* as the heart of sin:

> *Hubris* is not one form of sin beside others. It is sin in its total form, namely... the turning toward one's self as the center of one's self and one's world. This turning toward one's self is not an act done by a special part of man, such as his spirit. Man's whole life, including his sensual life, is spiritual... Its main symptom is that man does not acknowledge his finitude... And man identifies his cultural creativity with divine creativity. He attributes infinite significance to his finite cultural creations, making

idols of them, elevating them into matters of ultimate concern. The divine answer to man's cultural *hubris* comes in the disintegration and decay of every great culture in the course of history.[102]

It's in the state of *hubris* that Tillich says humans are taken from a positive "natural self-affirmation" of themselves into a "destructive self-elevation" of themselves. Or said another way, it's natural and healthy for humans to create and express their inner purposes, talents, and desires. However, if these creations are not seen as the finite, limited expressions they are, then one risks placing too much value on one's self and one's creations, thus increasing personal and social estrangement. The natural outcome of this ego-centered approach to life is to view others and the world simply as things to be used for one's own gratification, without true concern for either. And this brings us to the third and final element of sin.

The third element of sin, concupiscence, Tillich describes as the "unlimited desire to draw the whole of reality into one's self. It refers to all aspects of man's relation to himself and his world. It refers to physical hunger as well as to sex, to knowledge as well as to power, to material wealth as well to spiritual values."[103] Tillich sees this element of sin clearly expressed in modern industrial society's unfettered and greedy abuse of nature and other people. He uses the terms "commodification" and "thingification" to express this human drive to conquer and consume as much as it can, without contemplating the consequences of such behavior.

One particular reality that consistently challenges the idea of there being a God is the existence of evil—in theological terms this is called *theodicy*. The problem is familiar to most people, and it can be summed up this way: How could a God that is perfect, loving, and all-powerful allow evil to exist? On the face of it, this is a valid question we can all understand and relate to. But like much we find in theology, it's an argument already based on faulty assumptions and misinterpretations. This is Tillich's assessment of it:

> If one is asked how a loving and almighty God can permit evil, one cannot answer in the terms of the question as it was asked. One must first insist on an answer to this question How could he permit sin?—a question which is answered the moment it is asked. Not permitting sin would mean not permitting freedom; this would deny the very nature of man, his finite freedom. Only after this answer can one describe evil as the structure of self-destruction which is implicit in the nature of universal estrangement.[104]

Tillich's basic point here is that, without freedom, humans would not be, well, "human." That might sound like a circular argument, but when we consider the other options we cannot deny its truth. Let's look at the idea of evil, and then the other two options we can envision which would diminish, or eliminate, evil in the world.

First, we could be like other animals and not have a moral concept of evil, thus living our lives defined largely by biological necessity (eating, drinking, hunting, etc.), i.e., *without the freedom* to control our destinies and reach beyond the given in our environment. Or, second, we could have a perfectly planned and controlled human society devoid of evil, but also *without the freedom* to risk a mistake or attain human creativity and expression beyond the given, i.e., we could live like automatons or subjects of an authoritarian state regulating all our behavior. Many modern novels and films depict this latter state of society— usually in dystopian imagery, since a perfectly planned society would almost certainly lead to authoritarian control of the population and a diminished sense of human freedom. George Orwell's famous novel *1984* is a perfect example of this.

With these considerations, it becomes clear that the evil we experience is just an innate part of reality that could not be done away with without seriously compromising the depth of our human experience. This same idea is commonly expressed when people say things like "you have to know pain to know pleasure," or "the shadow does not exist without the light." In Chinese philosophy this is expressed in the concept of the *yin* and *yang* of life. With freedom comes risk and opportunity, and risk and opportunity often lead to evil.

As one could probably guess by now, just as he does not believe in the existence of a being called God, Tillich also does not believe in the existence of a being called the devil. The devil is simply a personified symbol of the destructive forces of existence, while God is a personified symbol of the creative forces of existence: "Destruction under the conditions of existential estrangement is not caused by some external force. It is not the work of special divine or demonic interferences, but it is the consequence of the structure of estrangement itself. One can describe this structure with a seemingly paradoxical term, 'structure of destruction.'"[105]

Here again, Tillich emphasizes his opposition to the idea of supernatural forces or supernatural beings—whether good or evil—controlling the fate of humans and the world. Instead, he uses the concept of "structures of destruction" to show that the inherent nature of human freedom is to sometimes contradict itself through acts leading to estrangement. This can be on an individual or social level, but the basic outcome is the same—through an act of freedom, humans lose the center and direction of their self and world by succumbing to evil. This happens not because some evil, demonic force or being is consciously controlling our existence, i.e., the devil. Rather, contained in the very nature of human freedom are forces and temptations pulling us toward disintegration rather than wholeness, healing, or reunion. Tillich sums up his answer to this disintegration and destruction: "In faith and love, sin is conquered because estrangement is overcome by reunion."[106]

7

SCIENCE, SPIRIT, AND THE "MULTIDIMENSIONAL UNITY OF LIFE": THE CASE AGAINST SUPERNATURALISM

"Of course, theology cannot rest on scientific theory. But it must relate its understanding of man to an understanding of universal nature, for man is a part of nature and statements about nature underlie every statement about him... Even if the questions about the relation of man to nature and to the universe could be avoided by theologians, they would still be asked by people of every place and time—often with existential urgency and out of cognitive honesty. And the lack of an answer can become a stumbling block for a man's whole religious life."[107]

In one of the most interesting, and often scientific, sections of his *Systematic Theology*, Tillich tackles the topic of humanity's relation to the planet and our evolution within the expansive, evolving life of the universe. The section is titled "The Multidimensionality Unity of Life," and in it his purpose is twofold: first, he wants to uphold the valid scientific criticisms against Christian supernaturalism (e.g., Creationism and Intelligent Design). Second, he wants to establish a viable understanding of Christianity that squares scientifically with how we know the world works. Ultimately, he wants to show that religion and science need not be in conflict; though they are related, integral parts of our human encounter with reality, they stand in two different dimensions of human inquiry and experience.

Beginning with the issue of evolution, Tillich immediately challenges the idea that a heavenly being (God) literally created the universe in six days about 6,000 years ago:

> Billions of years may have passed before the inorganic realm permitted the appearance of objects in the organic dimension, and millions of years before the organic realm permitted the appearance of a being with language. Again, it took tens of thousands of years before the being with the power of language became the historical man whom we know as ourselves.[108]

Before Tillich's death in 1965, we already had vast scientific evidence supporting the basic theories of evolution, and today that knowledge has grown considerably. So he makes this following statement to address the millions of people who still try to use the small holes in our scientific knowledge to support their supernatural views on creation. Forcefully challenging this "God of the gaps" theory, which he saw even amongst his own religious peers, Tillich states:

> Some theologians argued for the existence of God on the basis of our ignorance of the genesis of the organic out of the inorganic; they asserted that the 'first cell' can be explained only in terms of a special divine interference. Obviously, biology had to reject the establishment of such supernatural causality and to attempt to narrow our ignorance about the conditions for the appearance of organisms—an attempt which has been largely successful.[109]

But the problem is this: even if scientists finally pinpoint the exact way organic life came into existence, Creationists and Intelligent Designers will still say that a supernatural being caused it to happen. In other words, they cannot imagine life without a supernatural being in the sky creating, and then controlling, life on earth through divine interference—even if such a belief is not rational, nor essential, to religion.

The complaint Creationists make over and over again is that if one accepts evolution as fact, then one must also accept that humans are no more important than other species. The common refrain is: "If evolution is correct, then we're no better than monkeys." In proclaiming this ridiculous notion, they exhibit an inability to see the difference between biological complexity, and moral and psychological complexity. So Tillich addresses the Creationists' mistaken beliefs in two ways: 1) he denies that humans were created in a supernatural act by a supernatural being, while still maintaining that 2) human life has a special significance to the universe because of its complexity and evolution beyond simpler forms of life:

> That which presupposes something else and adds to it is by so much the richer. Historical man adds the historical dimension to all other dimensions which are presupposed and contained in his being. He is the highest grade from the point of view of valuation, presupposing that the criterion of such value judgment is the power of a being to include a maximum number of potentialities in one living actuality. . . Man is the highest being within the realm of our experience, but he is by no means the most perfect.[110]

Tillich's basic point is that humanity contains more dimensions of existence within it than any other species. The dimensions again are: inorganic, organic, psychological, historical, and spiritual. The dimensions overlap in some areas, and this is why Tillich is correct to point out that we cannot fully understand where the dimensions start and stop:

> If we define man as that organism in which the dimension of spirit is dominant, we cannot fix a definite point at which he appeared on earth. It is quite probable that for a long period the fight of the dimensions was going on in animal bodies which were anatomically physiologically similar to those which are ours as historical man, until the conditions were given for that leap which brought about the dominance of the dimension of the spirit.[111]

Tillich's basic point is that evolution is a long, gradual process devoid of any supernatural acts, and this process remains open to new dimensions arising in ourselves and other beings. In theological terms, Tillich would describe this as the process of God's creativity. Or said another way, it is the Ground of our Being going out from itself in resistance to the destructive forces of existence and creating something new in the universe that was previously out of reach of human cognition or experience.

The dimension which allows us to consciously grasp and shape our world in an intentional way Tillich calls "spirit." He describes the slow, open-ended process of spirit developing in humanity:

> Under special conditions the dimension of inner awareness, or the psychological realm, actualizes within itself another dimension, that of the personal-communal or the 'spirit.'

> Within reach of present human experience, this has happened only in man. The question of whether it has happened anywhere else in the universe cannot yet be answered positively or negatively.[112]

For Tillich, "spirit" is a dimension of human life that can be experienced and discussed, but it is not—as is commonly believed—a thing that "exists." Or said another way, "spirit is the power of animation itself and not a part added to the organic system."[113] The same can be said about "soul": "These considerations reject implicitly the doctrine that at a precise moment of the evolutionary process God in a special act added an 'immortal soul' to an otherwise complete human body."[114] In short, there is no such thing as either a spirit or a soul—these are simply concepts that express a dimension of human experience and human life. And since Tillich defines spirit as "the union of power and meaning," we can say that the dimension of spirit is what makes humans the most complex species. Within our experience, only our species is able to unite these two forces to create something new and spiritually conscious out of the givenness of the world—at least as far as we currently know.

Having said that we are the most complex species, we must now address the moral implications of this. Tillich alludes to it in the earlier quote when he says that, as a species, we are "by no means the most perfect." In order to understand what he means by this we have to distinguish between two things: *value based on complexity* (his way of saying that some species contain more dimensions than others), and *value based on morality* (his way of saying that a being is essentially what it is supposed to be).

The concept of value based on complexity is exemplified in the fact that humans include more dimensions than any other species—beyond the inorganic, organic dimensions, and psychological dimensions, we add to it the historical. and spiritual dimensions. This complexity gives us the freedom to choose our destinies and express ourselves in ways other species cannot. But there is a price to be paid for this complexity.

As we've encountered throughout Tillich's writing, the basic reality accompanying human choice and freedom is existential estrangement: from ourselves, from others and nature, and from the Ground of our Being (God). In other words, freedom comes with the price of making choices—and sometimes choosing things that tear us away from becoming what we are essentially supposed to be. This is why Tillich says we are the "highest" species in terms of our complexity, but we are not the most "perfect" species. In other words, we are not as morally perfect as other species, though we are certainly more complex in our experience of life's dimensions.

Humans are free to actualize their potentiality and spirit—using their *power* to discover and express *meaning*—and become what they essentially, or ought, to be. But they are also free to waste their potentiality and contradict their essential nature, by avoiding or rebelling against the positivity and depth of their existence. These two options make us internally split between the *ought* of our existence and the *is* of our existence. While other animals may not have the depth of experience with the world that we do because they are not as complex, they do nonetheless exist as they are meant to exist, i.e., they are not internally split and thus do not face the same moral threats we do. For instance, humans are free to destroy their world—which they are quite effectively and efficiently doing right now—while nonhuman animals do not have this freedom.

Tillich describes the complexity of the moral situation when he speaks of the relative completeness of humanity versus the relative incompleteness of other animals:

> Man is the creature in which the ontological elements are complete. They are incomplete in all creatures, which (for this very reason) are called 'subhuman.' Subhuman does not imply less perfection than in the case of the human. On the contrary, man as the essentially threatened creature cannot compare with the natural perfection of the subhuman creatures. Subhuman points to a different ontological level, not to a different degree of perfection.[115]

Here, Tillich expresses the moral "perfection" of other species. He then even goes even further by emphasizing the incredible importance of the "lowest" dimension of life, namely, the inorganic. And this raises the following question: why does he place so much importance on the material world (and the inorganic structures which compose it), when almost every other theologian does exactly the opposite? Very simply, all the other "advanced" dimensions of life (biological, historical, psychological, and spiritual) are completely dependent on the inorganic: "the inorganic dimension has a preferred position among the dimensions in so far as it is the first condition for the actualization of every other dimension. This is why all realms of being would dissolve were the basic condition provided by the constellation of inorganic structures to disappear."[116]

We exist and have biological, psychological, historical, and spiritual complexity because we are dependent on the so-called "lower" dimensions: the inorganic and the organic. Without the basic inorganic and organic structures of life, humanity would simply not exist. It's a simple scientific point to make, but since most past and modern theologians are so other-worldly— focusing almost exclusively on the afterlife, and thus relegating our relationship to the natural world as relatively meaningless or only incidental—Tillich's insight here is quite important. And it makes his theology highly significant for understanding and addressing modern humanity's problematic relationship with nature (see my previous book on Tillich and environmental ethics for more on this subject).[117]

Tillich's belief in the natural world's importance for supporting and further developing our species is only the beginning though. If we are to consider nature as rooted in God's ongoing creativity and as a vital part of life as a unified whole, then we have to also consider nature's value in ways that transcend our limited human concerns. In theological language, we have to consider the natural world's place within the context of "salvation":

> The problem is most urgent when Christian theology deals with the fall and the salvation of the world. Does 'world' refer to the human race alone? And, if so, can the human race be separated from other beings? Where is the boundary line in the general biological development; where is the boundary line in the development of the individual man? Is it possible to separate the nature which belongs to him through his body from universal nature? Does the unconscious realm of man's personality belong to nature or to man? Does the collective unconscious admit of the isolation of the individual from the other individuals and from the whole of the living substance? . . .Here theology should learn from modern naturalism, which at this point can serve as an introduction to a half-forgotten theological truth. What happens in the microcosm happens by mutual participation in the macrocosm, for being itself is one.[118]

With these far-reaching ideas on the depth and interconnectedness of our relationship to ourselves, nature, and other life forms—as well as salvation being a potentially universal phenomenon—we now turn to the heart of Tillich's theology: Jesus and his message. It's here we'll begin to find answers to the three questions posed at the beginning of the book: *Why am I here on earth?; how can I live my life in the most meaningful way?; and what does life ultimately mean?*

8

JESUS AS "THE CHRIST," "NEW BEING," AND "FINAL REVELATION"

"Christianity was born, not with the birth of the man who is called 'Jesus,' but in the moment in which one of his followers was driven to say to him, 'Thou art the Christ.' And Christianity will live as long as there are people who repeat this assertion. For the [revelatory] event on which Christianity is based has two sides: the fact which is called 'Jesus of Nazareth' and the reception of this fact by those who received him as the Christ."[119]

One thing I think most people fail to recognize is that Jesus never intended to establish a religion, let alone one based on the worship of himself. It's abundantly clear that Jesus fought against the idea of idols during his entire ministry, so why would he want to be made an idol himself? Unfortunately, what one sees and hears in most Christian churches today is exactly this—worship of the man Jesus.

For Tillich, this worship of Jesus is a major distortion in modern Christianity. It's a distortion so extreme that Tillich uses the word "demonic" to describe it. Remember that his use of this word always goes back to the following: the human elevation of something finite and transitory into ultimate significance. Therefore, by making Jesus the object of worship, modern Christian churches have created yet another idol—the exact opposite of what Jesus intended when he accepted the title "Christ." But what exactly does "Christ" mean? Before we address these questions, let's first take a look at the name "Jesus Christ":

> One must clearly see that Jesus Christ is not an individual name, consisting of a first and a second name, but that it is the combination of an individual name—the name of a certain man who lived in Nazareth between the years 1 and 30—with the title 'the Christ,' expressing in the mythological tradition a special figure with a special function... Therefore, the name Jesus Christ must be understood as 'Jesus who is called the Christ,' or 'Jesus who is the Christ,' or 'Jesus as the Christ,' or 'Jesus the Christ.'[120]

In biblical times, to say someone was "the Christ" meant they served the specific function of revealing an ultimate truth and, through this revelation of truth, of offering healing to a sick and estranged world (salvation). In Tillich's own terminology, the

Christ's function was to reveal himself as the "New Being," the bringer of a new eon that would conquer the corrupt, exploitative one he witnessed. Explaining how Jesus attained the title of Christ, as well as the consequences of this, Tillich says that

> Jesus became the Christ by conquering the demonic forces which tried to make him demonic by tempting him to claim ultimacy for his finite nature. These forces, often represented by his own disciples, tried to induce him to avoid sacrificing of himself as a medium of revelation. They wanted him to avoid the cross (cf. Matthew, chapter 16). They tried to make him an object of idolatry.[121]

As Tillich expresses it, one of the key requisites for becoming the Christ is sacrificing one's life to reveal the ultimate truth you are pointing to, or revealing. But many would ask, does the Christ really have to sacrifice his life? Remembering back to Chapter 3, when we discussed heteronomy, if a finite person or institution tries to impose itself on other people through its power and status, then it becomes just another idol seeking to be worshipped for its own ego-gratification and power. Tillich sums this up by talking of the temptation of idolatry that the Christ faced and how he became the "final revelation" by conquering this temptation:

> Heteronomy is the authority claimed or exercised by a finite being in the name of the

> infinite. Final revelation does not make such a claim and cannot exercise such a power. If it did, it would become demonic and cease to be final revelation. Far from being heteronomous and authoritarian, final revelation liberates. 'He who believes in me does not believe in *me*,' says Jesus in the Fourth Gospel, destroying any heteronomous interpretation of his divine authority.[122]

Had Jesus used his influence as the Christ to establish himself as some powerful political personality or cultic idol to be revered and worshipped—such as a Roman emperor might—he would have become simply another mortal claiming to be of infinite significance *in and of himself*. But this is not what he did. Instead, he sacrificed his bodily existence to point beyond himself to God, the Ground of Being.

For Tillich, it was through his actions and the sacrifice of his life that *the Christ represents to humanity what God intends humanity to be*. In short, the being and actions of Jesus unveil how people should relate to themselves, others, and the world in order to overcome the estrangement that mars all these relationships in existence. Tillich sums it up this way: Christ "represents to those who live under the conditions of existence what man essentially is and therefore ought to be under these conditions."[123]

The Christ's mission was to uncover humanity's essential (true) nature within its existential (distorted) nature. And since God is not a person, but is instead the very ground of

Being, any understanding of the statement "what God intends humanity to be" is paradoxical ("outside of ordinary experience"). And this is why Tillich underscores the point: "The paradox of the Christian message is that in one personal life essential manhood has appeared under the conditions of existence without being conquered by them."[124] Tillich elaborates this when he emphasizes the paradox between Christ being fully human and yet being fully transparent to the divine:

> The paradoxical character of his being consists in the fact that, although he has finite freedom under the conditions of time and space, he is not estranged from the ground of his being (God)... Even in the extreme situation of despair about his messianic work, he cries out to God who has forsaken him. In the same way the biblical picture shows no trace of *hubris* or self-elevation... In the critical moment in which Peter first calls him the Christ, he combines the acceptance of this title with the acceptance of his violent death, including the warning to his disciples not to make his messianic function public.[125]

In all his statements about Jesus, Tillich emphasizes that Jesus was fully human. He knows he must die, he experiences loneliness, doubt (even on the cross), a lack of a definite home, a deep concern for the miseries of the masses, and the scorn of the authorities—and yet he accepts these people even though he will be rejected by them. Highlighting Jesus' humanity, Tillich even makes the interesting point "that Jesus was involved in the tragic element of guilt, in so far as he made his enemies inescapably guilty."[126]

In spite of Jesus' participation in the ambiguities and distortions of life, his essential humanity shined through every one of his words, deeds, and sufferings. And because he made his essential humanity clear to those around him, Tillich says Jesus was transparent to the divine mystery.[127] It's in reference to this power of Jesus' being that Tillich speaks of him as "truth," and this takes us back to the philosophical concept of *logos*:

> The Fourth Gospel says of him that he *is* truth, but this does not mean that he *has* omniscience or absolute certainty. He *is* the truth in so far as his being—the New Being in him—conquers the untruth of existential estrangement. . . Finitude implies openness to error, and error belongs to the participation of the Christ in man's existential predicament.[128]

According to Tillich, it was Jesus' acceptance of the cross that is "the decisive test of his unity with God, of his complete transparency to the ground of being." This is what makes Tillich call the revelation of Christ "final":

> The first and basic answer theology must give to the question of the finality of the revelation in Jesus as the Christ is the following: a

> revelation is final if it has the power of negating itself without losing itself. . . He who is the bearer of final revelation must surrender his finitude—not only his life but also his finite power and knowledge and perfection. In doing so, he affirms that is the bearer of final revelation (the 'Son of God' in classical terms). He becomes completely transparent to the mystery he reveals. But, in order to be able to surrender himself completely, he must possess himself completely. And only he can possess—and therefore surrender—himself completely who is united with the ground of his being and meaning without separation and disruption. . .[129]

Now if Tillich says that a religion is witness to a "final revelation," it would be natural to assume that he sees Christianity as superior to other religions. But Tillich is quick to point out that Christianity, as a religion, has no superiority over other religions. This is why he says that "When contemporary theology rejects the name 'religion' for Christianity, it is in the line of New Testament thought. The coming of the Christ is not the foundation of a new religion but the transformation of the old state of things."[130] And this is why so much of modern-day Christianity is off-the-mark when it tries to establish itself as the "one and only true religion." In the end, Christianity's claim is this: it is not final or universal as a religion, but it is witness to what is final and universal, i.e., the Christ, the one who shows us what God intends us to be, and who helps us overcome the existential estrangement keeping us from union with the ground, power, and meaning of our being.

As we can see, Tillich's understanding of the Christ is quite different than what we hear in most churches today. Christians now often express his mission by saying that Jesus "died for our sins." The problem is that such a statement is confusing and misleading, bringing up more questions that it does answers. Why would Jesus' death take away my sins? What exactly are my sins? And how do I know if the murder of Jesus really does take away my sin? Answering such questions these days is not so easy, because the Bible is not an instruction manual laying out a list of every sin. And even if it did, would avoiding each and every one of these sins necessarily bring us more joy in life, or bring us into better communion with ourselves, others, the world, and God?

Tillich says sin is not disobedience to a moral or religious commandment, but is rather any expression of our estrangement from God, the Ground of our Being. Thus, one does not find healing and salvation by simply avoiding certain "sinful" acts and by obeying moral or religious authorities. In fact, as Tillich often pointed out, the more one feels compelled to follow rules and commandments, the more one really exhibits estrangement from one's essential, or true, being. We often see this when strict adherence to moral and religious laws leads to increased estrangement and judgment between adherents of different religions—or even more estrangement between the followers of the same religion! As Tillich sees it, when we are in touch with our essential natures we naturally express the good, the true, and the virtuous without feeling compelled to follow laws and rules. And we do this not because of the promise of some future reward, but because doing the good is the reward itself.

Another problem with modern-day Christianity's understanding of Jesus is that most Christians believe what makes him special is his seemingly supernatural powers. Without these powers—and the truth of the miracle stories based on these powers—Christians feel their faith would fall apart. For if Jesus did not have these supernatural powers, would he then really have the ability to lead people to a heavenly place after death? To Tillich, this reasoning betrays a total misunderstanding of Christian faith.

The point of Christianity is not simply to transform one's personal beliefs and behavior in order to gain admittance into a heavenly realm through the supernatural powers of Jesus or God. Rather, instead of being concerned with escaping this life for a "heavenly" life—a reality we do not even know—one's faith should be vitally concerned with transforming this life and the current reality we do know and live in. Tillich describes this drive for transformation as the drive for a "new reality" beyond the current one characterized by estrangement: "New reality presupposes an old reality; and this old reality... is the state of estrangement of man and his world from God."[131]

Rather than focus on whether or not Jesus had supernatural powers granted to him by a being called God, we should instead focus on the meaning his being has for our own lives.

Tillich puts it this way: "God's presence and power should not be sought in the supranatural interference in the ordinary course of events but in the power of the New Being to overcome the self-destructive consequences of existential estrangement in and through the created structures of reality."[132] A statement like this—which emphasizes the importance of using one's faith to transform historical existence for the better—directly counters the modern fundamentalist view we see summed up in the common religious-escapist bumper sticker: "Not of this world." In this latter type of thinking, existence and the world itself are corrupted, evil things to be tolerated as necessary. But they are not to be enjoyed, reverenced, or even necessarily bettered through social, economic, ecological, political, or racial justice.

This is the strength of Tillich's interpretation of the Christian message, because here we see the regenerative and transformative power of the New Being as applicable to all realms of existence; the love and healing manifested through Christ's being has deep significance for our personal, economic, political, and ecological relationships. If our understanding of Christ limits our concerns only to ourselves, or somehow neglects the importance of justice in this world, then we have completely missed the message of the New Being: "The Messiah does not save individuals in a path leading out of historical existence; he is to transform historical existence. The individual enters a new reality which embraces society and nature. . . the New Being does not demand the sacrifice of finite being; instead, it fulfills all finite being by conquering its estrangement."[133] In short, if one's faith does not lead to a serious concern for all realms of historical existence and all people, then one's faith is stunted.

Now, if you believe that life can be explained only in scientific-materialist terms and that anything "religious" or "spiritual" is simply misguided, then the idea of a new reality at work in the world may make little sense, or seem ridiculous—especially if one thinks this new reality is some supernatural "thing" that exists (like a material soul or spirit). On the other hand, if you are a Christian fundamentalist who thinks there are actual supernatural forces at work in the world and that our "real" life exists beyond the grave, then the idea of a new reality at work in the world is of limited value. Why? Because rather than leading to a belief in the transformative power of the New Being to change every realm of historical and material existence, it instead leads to a belief in magic, the unimportance of this world, and an obsession with what happens to one's "soul" after death.

In the end, these two options—the strictly scientific-materialist, as well as the supernatural-religious—fail to see anything outside their own limited assumptions. In the first instance, the scientific-materialist viewpoint sees nothing beyond physical and/or chemical explanations for life—sometimes with its own almost religious-like faith. In this view, life is nothing but a purposeless chance event that can be reduced to purely scientific explanations, leading Tillich to call it an "ontology of death." Here, analyzing and reducing everything down to the inorganic lifelessness of the universe takes a metaphysical precedence over the immediate presence and seeming miracle of life on earth. On the other hand, the supernatural-religious view demands even more strict and limiting beliefs, because it puts forth ideas and concepts that often run counter to how we know the natural world works. Both minimize the importance of our life on this earth, and thus Tillich sees them as offering impoverished, sometimes dangerous, worldviews.

It's important to emphasize that the scientific way of understanding and explaining the world cannot, and should not, be thrown out—a mistake many fundamentalists make. But it should also be emphasized that the strictly scientific way of understanding life should not be envisioned as the only other alternative to fundamentalist-supernaturalist belief. So what is the other alternative? Tillich calls it "belief-ful realism," and it's a stance towards life uniting both a religious and a scientific sensibility.

In this vision of life, there is the recognition of an ultimate or religious meaning beneath the surface of all political, economic, artistic, cultural, philosophical, and scientific endeavors. And such realism means we take seriously all dimensions of life, including the science and the significance its discoveries have on our self-understanding. Beyond this, it means we should also recognize the self-transcending nature of life and the impossibility for humans to comprehensively explain life processes in only chemical and physical terms. This is why Tillich claims words like "miracle," "mystery," and "paradox" still have meaning for us today—if they are properly defined and understood.

Terms like "paradox" are difficult for the modern mind to comprehend and accept because it doesn't fall neatly into either strict scientific or supernatural-religious understandings of life.

As Tillich puts it, "That is paradoxical which contradicts the *doxa*, the opinion which is based on the whole of ordinary human experience, including the empirical and the rational..."[134] We can see that the paradoxical nature of Christianity is problematic for people today because it contains ideas and concepts about life that often transcend the two most common options we've been given to understand and explain the world. To the scientific mind, such paradoxical ideas and concepts are simply wrong because they can't be explained only in materialist terms. And to the fundamentalist mind these paradoxes are meaningful only if we believe in supernatural events and a supernatural realm. Unfortunately, both of these belief systems are limited in their understanding of life's complexity.

Many people also point out that because of our lack of historical knowledge of Jesus, it's very difficult to reconstruct exactly who he was. Tillich is in total agreement with this assessment, citing scholars' quests to find the "historical Jesus" as evidence that

> the attempt of historical criticism to find the empirical truth about Jesus of Nazareth was a failure. The historical Jesus, namely, the Jesus behind the symbols of his reception as the Christ, not only did not appear but receded farther and farther with every new step... The reports about Jesus of Nazareth are those of Jesus as the Christ, given by persons who had received him as the Christ. Therefore, if one

> tries to find the real Jesus behind the picture of Jesus as the Christ, it is necessary critically to separate the elements which belong to the factual side of the event from the elements which belong to the receiving side.[135]

In other words, what we have is a historical picture of Jesus as he was received and reported on by his followers, namely, as the Christ. What we don't have is a solid historical picture of who Jesus was to those who did not receive him as the Christ. And this again brings to light the issue of whether Jesus was human or divine.

The discussion of whether Jesus was human or divine has largely rested on the assumption that to be "divine" means to be a supernatural being. As we've seen throughout Tillich's writings, this is a misunderstanding of the word. For Tillich, to be divine means to be transparent to God, the Ground of our Being. And if God is understood as the Ground and true nature of our being—which humans manifest in the moral act of becoming what we are supposed to be—then it does make sense to speak of Jesus as "divine." Does this mean he had supernatural powers and could perform acts that ran counter to the natural laws governing the universe? We simply don't know. And from Tillich's perspective, this is not even the issue.

Unfortunately, most people see Jesus in these starkly contrasting terms: he either had supernatural powers and was divine, or he didn't have these powers and thus was not divine; both of these alternatives miss the point. So Tillich says we should not use the term "divine nature" when describing Jesus:

"Jesus as the Christ is the personal unity of a divine and a human nature must be replaced by the assertion that in Jesus as the Christ the eternal unity of God and man has become historical reality."[136] Tillich suggests using terms such as "eternal God-man-unity" or "Eternal God-Manhood." The basic point is that, whatever terms we use to describe Jesus, in his life he expressed both complete humanity (suffering, anxiety, doubts, etc.) as well as complete divinity (transparency to the Ground of Being, or God). He was a fully human being, but he was also something more. Again, this is the paradox of Christianity.

Uncertainties about who Jesus truly was have been enduring throughout history. And this uncertainty is why Tillich sees faith as always characterized by the elements of doubt, daring, and ultimately, courage:

> The affirmation that Jesus is the Christ is an act of faith and consequently of daring courage. It is not an arbitrary leap into darkness but a decision in which elements of immediate participation and therefore certitude are mixed with elements of strangeness and therefore incertitude and doubt. But doubt is not the opposite of faith; it is an element of faith. Therefore, there is no faith without risk.[137]

Tillich even goes so far as to say that we cannot guarantee the name of the person we call the Christ was "Jesus," though we are almost certain it was. It is simply another historical question scholars have brought to light in their discussions of the "historical Jesus." These uncertainties naturally bring into question the nature and risk of faith. And this is where Tillich makes one of his most important statements about faith:

> The problem is: Exactly what can faith guarantee? And the inevitable answer is that faith can guarantee only its own foundation, namely, the appearance of that reality which has created the faith. This reality is the New Being, who conquers existential estrangement and thereby makes faith possible. . . No historical criticism can question the immediate awareness of those who find themselves transformed into the state of faith. . . one must say that participation, not historical argument, guarantees the reality of the event upon which Christianity is based. It guarantees a personal life in which the New Being has conquered the old being. But it does not guarantee his name to be Jesus of Nazareth. Historical doubt concerning the existence of someone with this name cannot be overruled. He might have had another name. (This is a historically absurd, but logically necessary, consequence of the historical method.) Whatever his name, the New Being was and is actual in this man.[138]

These words affirm Tillich's notion that faith is much larger than simply belief in statements and stories which may or may not be historically or scientifically true—the common, albeit distorted, understanding of faith. This faulty understanding of fait—as belief in things that may or may not be true—will always be open to the changing circumstances of historical knowledge and criticism.

Tillich's understanding of faith as an existential position towards life itself is largely immune to such historical uncertainties. Why? Because faith as an existential position is based on an inner shift in one's relationship to others, one's self, the world, and the meaning of life itself—not on whether something did or did not happen in the past. And when one is grasped by faith and this transforms one's being on the deepest level of understanding and action, no historical changes can take this away. *This is why Tillich is famously quoted as saying that his faith would remain intact even if it were proven Jesus never existed!*

In the end, the person grasped by faith is guaranteed one thing: their own deeply transformed stance towards existence itself. And the basis of this transformation goes back to Christianity's paradoxical claim: through the life of a finite human who was able to conquer guilt, sin, temptation, judgment, and estrangement, God unveiled to us what we should be. When a person is grasped by this power and works toward actualizing it in their life, they experience what Tillich calls the "New Being." The New Being causes one to strive for a life of love, with the ultimate goal of establishing reunion with all of reality, including one's self, others, nature, and the Ground of Being (God).

I emphasize it as a striving because, as noted throughout this book, the human ability to overcome existential estrangement is always fragmentary, ambiguous, and transitory. And though Tillich sees this power to overcome estrangement as completely and uniquely present in the Christ, he insists that such power is available, present, and/or actual in people of all faiths—as well as in people who have no relationship to religion at all. This is why he sees the life and meaning of Jesus as universally valid. And when he describes how the power of the New Being is actualized personally in one's life, he again emphasizes the transformative power of deep questioning and introspection:

> If, however, the question—What can I do to experience the New Being?—is asked with existential seriousness, the answer is implied in the question, for existential seriousness is evidence of the impact of the Spiritual Presence upon an individual. He who is ultimately concerned about his state of estrangement and the possibility of reunion with the ground and aim of his being is already in the grip of the Spiritual Presence. In this situation the question, What shall I do to receive the divine Spirit? is meaningless because the real answer is already given and any further answer would distort it.[139]

Now that I've covered Tillich's basic understanding of the Christ and the meaning of his being and mission, I'd like to discuss what humans experience when they are grasped by it. Or, put in the form of a question: What is the relationship between faith and salvation?

9

SALVATION AS HEALING

If you were to ask the average person on the street what salvation means in the context of Christianity, I'm willing to bet their answer would go something like this: Salvation means that, through my asking for forgiveness for all the bad personal acts ("sins") I've committed throughout my life, I have been forgiven by a being called God, through the crucifixion of his "son" Jesus, and I will be granted eternal entrance into a place called heaven after death. As we all know, the opposite of salvation is condemnation, whereby you're not forgiven by God for your sins and you spend an eternity in pain and torment—overseen by an evil creature named the devil—in a place called hell.

Such an understanding of salvation raises a few serious questions: What is the ultimate criterion determining who gets forgiven and who doesn't? And since we have to be honest and say that we really don't know objectively what this criterion is, how can we be sure we've been personally forgiven and saved from hell? If I've lived a life almost devoid of love and filled with terrible, horrific acts against myself, others, and the world, will simply asking for forgiveness at the end of my life guarantee my entrance to heaven? What if I was born, lived, and died without ever hearing about Jesus; am I doomed to hell?

If you asked these questions to a fundamentalist, they would tell you that all you have to do is believe that Jesus died for your sins, ask him into your heart, and then obey the Christian commandments to gain entry into heaven—and this entrance into heaven is the ultimate point of being Christian in the first place. To Tillich, this explanation of salvation is a vast oversimplification of the Christian message. The questions of Jesus' mission and the meaning of salvation should instead take us back to the paradox of Christianity, namely, that in an actual finite human life the destructive and alienating elements of existence were overcome through love.

In numerous biblical stories, we have the picture of a man offering personal healing to those in need of it, whether bodily, spiritually, or morally. On a larger social scale, we also see Jesus offering economic and political healing to a society corrupted by systemic exploitation and domination over the weak and powerless—specifically, domination by the heads of the Roman Empire and by exploitative, legalistic forms of Judaism. In Jesus' eyes, both of these groups only served to increase humanity's estrangement from itself and God. In place of this, Jesus offers what Tillich calls, paradoxically, the "law of love": "The law of love is the ultimate law because it is the negation of law; it is absolute because it concerns everything concrete."[140] In other words, the law of love stands against all forms of exploitation, dehumanization, and "power over" relationships because it does not see humans in an abstract way. Every concrete need in every instance of suffering is seen for what it is: demanding of love and justice.

According to Tillich, only a person morally centered and in full command and expression of their essential self can offer the radical healing and transformation we encounter in the biblical stories of Jesus. In other words, only a fully realized, essentialized self—as opposed to an existentially estranged self—can offer salvation, i.e., healing. But to make such a statement brings us to a fundamental issue surrounding the very concept of salvation, namely, the basic meaning of the term. And, more importantly, how do we participate in this salvation?

Like so many words in religion, the word salvation has become distorted to the point where it now means something completely other than what it should. We know this by simply looking at the root of the word; "salvation" comes from the Latin word *salvus*, which means "to heal or make whole." Thus, Tillich defines salvation theologically in this way: ". . . healing means reuniting that which is estranged, giving a center to what is split, overcoming the split between God and man, man and his world, man and himself. Out of this interpretation of salvation, the concept of the New Being has grown. Salvation is reclaiming from the old and transferring into the New Being."[141]

As we can see, Tillich's definition of salvation is quite different from how most people conceive of it today, namely, as a cosmic, individual deliverance of one's "soul" to a place called heaven. Tillich is quite clear in his opposition to this understanding of the word: ". . . salvation is not the transference of man from the material world to a so-called spiritual world."[142] Therefore, he laments that traditional theological doctrines "have mostly lost the original power of the idea of salvation, its cosmic meaning which includes nature, man as a whole, and society. . . Salvation is basically a cosmic event: the world is saved."[143]

Throughout history people have had various ideas about an enduring part of themselves that will live on after death. Often seen as a material, or even immaterial "soul" or "spirit," this entity supposedly lives on in another realm of existence after one's death (heaven or hell), or perhaps transfers into another living being through reincarnation (e.g., in Buddhism). But, as we know, the Christian tradition has largely been defined by a belief that one's soul is judged by a being called God, and then either sent to a place called heaven or hell.

Tillich calls this black-and-white, supernatural vision a "twofold eternal destiny," in which there is nothing between heaven and hell— either one is "eternally saved" or one is "eternally condemned." In this line of thinking, to be saved one must live a moral life, avoid sinful behavior, "ask Jesus into their heart," and follow the Christian commandments. To Tillich, this is not an accurate or biblical account of salvation. Among many other problems, this belief is based on a simplistic understanding of morality as "good behavior" and the "following of commandments," rather than on becoming the centered, loving, non-judgmental person the Ground of Being

(God) intends humans to become by overcoming estrangement in all dimensions of our existence (social, economic, personal, political, ecological, etc.).

Speaking philosophically, Tillich also points out how the idea of heaven and hell contradicts Augustine's "great anti-dualistic statement" that "being as being is good." In other words, if the very creation and existence of the universe is seen as a positive, creative thing (a basic Christian tenet found in Genesis), then nothing in existence can be entirely bad or evil. This is not to say there isn't evil, as all of us are a mixture of both good and bad. But summing up his opposition to the literal idea of a heaven and a hell, Tillich says:

> If being as being is good... nothing that is can become completely evil... The doctrine of the unity of everything in divine love and in the Kingdom of God deprives the symbol of hell of its character as 'eternal damnation.' This doctrine does not take away the seriousness of the condemning side of the divine judgment, the despair in which the exposure of the negative is experienced. But it does take away the absurdities of a literal understanding of heaven and hell and also refuses to permit the confusion of eternal destiny with an everlasting state of pain or pleasure... Even the saint remains a sinner and needs forgiveness and even the sinner is a saint in so far as he stands under divine forgiveness.[144]

For Tillich, all of reality is a unified whole, and none of us can claim complete goodness, nor complete separation, from the rest of humanity and the natural world that supports our existence. In addition to this, we know that all humans are a made up of a constellation of factors over which we have only limited conscious influence. For instance, we have economic, political, and social forces directing our lives; unconscious motivations that we feel but sometimes don't fully control or understand (psychology); and even anti-social neurological "wiring" that is found in some people (biology). All of this makes it impossible to say that "I" am completely in control of myself, or that I am entirely separate from all other people. Simply put, our personal identity is composed of many factors somewhat out of our control, and we should take this into account when discussing morality and salvation.

What we should not do, as Tillich emphasizes, is use these elusive factors to entirely excuse or justify evil or anti-social behavior. Instead, we should use this knowledge to begin understanding and treating people with a more realistic, scientifically-based frame of reference. By doing this, we might begin to see certain people less as "criminals" or "bad," and instead as victims of economic, political, or neurological/biological forces that make them more prone to so-called "bad behavior." Modern scientific studies linking aberrant neurology to anti-social tendencies (crime) and/or substance abuse (drugs and alcohol) are just two examples of this.

At its root, the twofold theory of heaven and hell that Tillich opposes is based on a faulty understanding of humanity. If we remember back to his understanding of life as a multidimensional unity, everything in existence is based on a complex interrelationship of organic and inorganic processes—devoid of any supernatural influences. But the twofold destiny presupposes "a radical separation of person from person and of the personal from the subpersonal."[145] Tillich proposes the opposite and says that every human destiny is tied up with every other human destiny. Moreover, we are also ultimately connected to all things in existence that aren't human (i.e., the "subpersonal"): animals, the natural world, and every other form of organic and inorganic matter in the universe. And this conviction is what led to his famous statement that "there is no salvation of man if there is no salvation of nature, for man is in nature and nature is in man."[146]

For Tillich, understanding the unity of existence has vast implications for how one's faith plays out. A person who sees him or herself spiritually-linked to others and the natural world—by virtue of being a part of the multidimensional unity of *all* life—is more apt to exhibit the behaviors we commonly associate with Christianity: tolerance, love, forgiveness, humility, compassion, and nurture, to name but a few. And this drastically widens how we understand the concept of salvation: "Man cannot claim that the infinite has entered the finite to overcome its existential estrangement in mankind alone. . . The interdependence of everything with everything else in the totality of being includes a participation of nature in history and demands a participation of the universe in salvation."[147] Thus, salvation is an on-going process that relates as much to nature as it does to humans.[148]

It's a rare thing to hear a Christian minister proclaim such a message, and Tillich was far ahead of his time in doing so. One can only imagine what the world be like if we started to hear such a message in the Christian churches—especially in a world threatened with possible ecological collapse. Long before what we now know as the "ecological age," Tillich defined human creations that desecrated nature as "structures of destruction." In doing so, he established theology as a field with the moral authority to critique all aspects of humanity and its relationship to itself and its world. His critiques of capitalism, nuclear power, war, art, quasi-religions, and political ideologies—among many other things—showed that theology should have something meaningful to say about all realms of human thought and action. The gravity of this is perhaps summed up no better than when he proclaims the following:

> Today it is man who has the power to blot himself out, and often he is so sorry that he has been made that he desires to withdraw from his humanity altogether. . . Can it be that the earth, fully conquered by man, will cease to be a place where man wants to live?[149]

A further problem with the twofold destiny theory (heaven and hell) is that, because God is not a being, object, or human, it's hard to speak of someone or something literally judging us after we die. Among many other problems, this idea raises the question of how a loving God could create, and then condemn, a good, moral person to an eternity of torment just because he or she didn't know about Jesus, or because he or she made a few bad decisions in life. Think of all the millions of people in the world who know very little about, or who have never even heard of, this person named Jesus. This, in fact, is one of Tillich's key challenges to the standard understanding of salvation, and he sums it up this way:

> If. . . the salvation to eternal life is made dependent upon the encounter with Jesus as the Christ and the acceptance of his saving power, only a small number of human beings will ever reach salvation. . . Only if salvation is understood as healing and saving power through the New Being in all history is the problem put on another level.[150]

For Tillich, the saving (healing) power of the Christ is also present in people who belong to other faiths than Christianity, and even in those who have no religion whatsoever. Wherever the effort is made to overcome estrangement through love, Tillich sees the presence of the New Being at work in persons and groups. He therefore calls some non-religious groups "latent Spiritual Communities," and they may be seen at work in civic, political, medical, educational, or any number of other organizations.

Those who claim Christianity as their spiritual home will consciously acknowledge this healing presence and power of the New Being, but this does not mean they have a monopoly on it. In short, salvation exists outside the Christian churches, too. In fact, Tillich believed that oftentimes the work of the New Being is seen more clearly in people outside of the churches than in those who consciously call themselves "Christian." This is the basis for his belief in the universality of salvation, as well as his distinction between the narrow and wider expressions of religion.

And again, since God cannot be seen as a thing or being that exists in a material sense, Tillich says it's also not possible to speak of each of us having an individual soul—because souls are not things that exist either. Rather, "soul" and "spirit" are terms we use to describe a dimension unique to human existence. They are symbols we've developed to denote the self-transcending part of our humanity—the part of ourselves we experience as being larger than our individual egos, or limited by our temporary space in time and history. And it's the "spirit-ual," "soul-ful," ecstatic experiences we are sometimes grasped by that reveals to us our connection with all persons, nature, and God. This experience might come, for example, when listening to music, when deeply in love, when in nature, or when viewing a poignant piece of art.

Tillich calls this self-transcending part of our life experience an encounter with the "Eternal Now," or the experience of God (the Eternal) within time:

> People who are never aware of this dimension lose the possibility of resting in the present... They are held by the past and cannot separate themselves from it, or they escape towards the future, unable to rest in the present. They have not entered the eternal rest which stops the

> flux of time and gives us the blessing of the present. Perhaps this is the most conspicuous characteristic of our period, especially in the western world and particularly in this country [America]. It lacks the courage to accept 'presence' because it has lost the dimension of the eternal.[151]

The eternal is present in each moment we are grasped by the ultimate meaning of our existence. Thus, for Tillich the eternal is both a *quantitative* fact about the infinite nature of time, but more so, it is a *qualitative* experience of the depth of life itself: "The eternal is not a future state of things. It is always present, not only in man (who is aware of it), but also in everything that has being within the whole of being."[152] The significance of this qualitative aspect of the eternal is that, when we are grasped by it, it has the power to change our relationship to life in all of its dimensions (psychological, social, historical, spiritual, ecological, etc.). So in Tillich's understanding of morality and salvation, we do the good and the virtuous not because of some reward in the future, such as an afterlife in a place called heaven. We do these things because, in the act of becoming our essential self, we experience the Eternal ("God" in terms of time) and the Ground of Being ("God" in terms of space).

In the end, becoming a morally-centered person is rewarded by an experience of the depth of life *in this existence* and, if he is correct about what happens after death, a reunion with the Ground of our Being (God) *after our existence*. Tillich would say this is our experience of salvation—the feeling of being accepted and supported by Being-Itself—in the midst of all the negativities of life. It is rooted in the feeling that we come from God and will return to God—the eternal Ground of everything that exists. If we experience this eternal quality in our lives, we are opened up to a sense that we are shaped by everything historically and biologically that has come before us, and that we will in some small way, help shape what comes after us; we have an experience of our ultimate significance to the evolution of the life process, however small we may sometimes feel.

Ultimately, salvation has to do with much more than just one's individual future in an afterlife, whether a heaven or a hell; salvation has everything to do with the here-and-now. And it also applies to the entire universe and not just to humans. That's why, for Tillich, it's impossible to envision a twofold destiny with every individual person separated from every other person, or from nature. This separation is a mythical fiction that should be done away with—as should the idea of heaven and hell being literal places that one goes to after death.

If we are to really understand Tillich's concept of salvation, we have to be prepared to ask ourselves this: if there were in fact a thing called a human soul, how could we understand it as completely "ours," when the borders between everything in existence—whether looked at inorganically, organically, historically, spiritually, or morally—are ever-moving, interrelated, and permeable? Tillich would answer, "we couldn't." For him, all beings participate universally in Being-Itself, or God. And this vision of life and the universe as a unified oneness is what brings us to the final chapter. Here, Tillich shares his vision of what might happen to us and our universe after death.

10

THE ETERNAL, AND IDEAS ON WHAT HAPPENS AFTER DEATH

> *"The destiny of the individual cannot be separated from the destiny of the whole in which it participates... The division of mankind into fulfilled and unfulfilled individuals, or into objects of predestination either to salvation or to condemnation, is existentially and, therefore, theologically, impossible."*[53]

No one who exists knows what happens to us after we die, and no one who exists ever will. In spite of this, ideas regarding life beyond the grave have always been of great concern and interest to humans. Tillich's views on the subject, though of course speculative like all others, are some of the most challenging, reasonable, and ultimately affirming ones you will encounter in any philosophy or theology.

If judged simply by the opening quote to this chapter, you can already see Tillich's strong opposition to the widely accepted fundamentalist belief in total salvation (heaven) versus total condemnation (hell). Tillich sees this black-and-white ideology as an erroneous and unbiblical distortion of the central Christian concept of salvation. He points out how this distorted version of salvation arose largely through the influence of Hellenistic (Greek) thought on Christianity, which emphasized a dualistic understanding of human destiny. In this philosophical strain there is a radical separation of person from person, and between people and nature.

To counter the idea of every person being completely separated from every other person and nature—while also countering the idea of heaven and hell as literally existing apart somewhere in other realms of the universe—Tillich shows that Christianity has strong theories and teachings on the universal participation of all of reality in an Eternal Life, or Eternal Memory, beyond death. The foundation for this belief of his, covered in Chapter 7, is seen in his anti-supernatural, scientifically-based description of life as a multidimensional unity. To sum up this idea of his, we can say that the universe is a vast but unified reality in which all elements of existence are connected; there is no separation of the universe into an earth, a heaven, and a hell. Heaven and hell are symbols and not actual locations in, or beyond, the universe.

Before jumping to any conclusions about what an eternal "life" might be like beyond our death, we have to understand Tillich's opposition to the idea of us literally having an individual soul that will live on forever when we die. In fact, Tillich points out how the idea of living on forever could itself be envisioned as a hell:

Many people... hope for a continuation of this life after death. They expect an endless future in which they may achieve or possess what has been denied them in this life. This is a prevalent attitude about the future, and also a very simple one. It denies that there *is* an end. It refuses to accept that we are creatures, that we come from the eternal ground of time and return to the eternal ground of time and have received a limited span of time as *our* time. It replaces eternity by endless future.

But endless future is without a final aim; it repeats itself and could well be described as an image of hell...

But the world, by its very nature, is that which comes to an end. If we want to speak in truth without foolish, wishful thinking, we should speak about the eternal that is neither timelessness nor endless time. The mystery of the future is answered in the eternal of which we may speak in images taken from time. But if we forget that the images are images, we fall into absurdities and self-deceptions. There is no time *after* time, but there is eternity *above* time.[154]

Eastern religions echo this in theories of reincarnation, where an endless continuation of life is an undesirable thing (samsara).

And if we were to compare Eastern thought with Tillich's, we would say that in the East the ultimate goal (nirvana or enlightenment) is to see through to the true nature of reality by overcoming the ignorance and attachments of our individual ego-consciousness. For Tillich, the ultimate goal (salvation) is to become our morally-centered, essential self by overcoming existential estrangement through faith and love. Though an entire book could be written solely on this subject, it's worth pointing out how there are many overlapping and complimentary elements in Western and Eastern ideas on what happens beyond death.

Tillich sees a problem in the idea of an eternal, individual soul because it fails to acknowledge that our personal existences (and thus self-identities) do, in fact, come to a mortal end. Many people simply don't want to accept this fact, and so they hold on to the idea of their self-identity (their "I") living on forever. Tillich clarifies that it is not our ego, or a personal soul, that participates in an eternal life when he compares the symbols of reincarnation (Eastern) and immortality (Western):

> reincarnation must be understood—similarly to immortality—as a symbol and not as a concept. It points to higher or lower forces which are present in every being and which fight each other to determine the individual's essentialization on a higher or lower level of fulfillment. One does not *become* an animal in the next incarnation, but unhumanized

> qualities may prevail in a human being's personal character and determine the quality of his essentialization.[155]

In this quote we first glimpse into the heart of Tillich's ideas on our destinies after death—a process he calls "essentialization." He defines this succinctly as the "elevation of the positive into Eternal Life." In other words, the positive elements of our being that we have cultivated in life are taken up into the Eternal, or God. And this is what connects the quality of our moral lives with what happens after we die. In other words, in the process of our essentialization there are varying degrees of fulfillment. And the degree to which we participate in the Eternal Memory of God is determined by what we made of ourselves in existence.

To sum up the process of essentialization, let me describe the two options we have in life by using extreme examples: First, we can strive for our essential self in existence—through love and faith—and seek to reunite with all of Being; find and actualize our moral center in the process; and thus experience the ultimate depth of life and existential healing, i.e., salvation. Alternatively, we can deny or turn away from our essential self; distort and destroy our moral center in the process; and thus fail to experience the depth of life and remain in the grips of existential estrangement, i.e., condemnation. Tillich explains it this way:

> Participation in the eternal life depends on a creative synthesis of a being's essential nature

> with what it has made of it in its temporal existence. In so far as the negative has maintained possession of it, it is exposed in its negativity and excluded from eternal memory. Whereas, in so far as the essential has conquered existential distortion its standing is higher in eternal life.[156]

In short, during our life we have the choice of using our moral freedom to become what God (the Ground of Being) intends us to be, or we can use our moral freedom to distort and turn away from God. The whole spiritual developmental process is, for Tillich, a movement away from this "existential estrangement" toward our "essential self." This movement is the moral act, in which we activate healing in all dimensions of existence through love and Ultimate Concern (faith). In this process God participates in our existence and we participate in God's continuing creativity.

As we've seen, for Tillich there is no total condemnation or total salvation after death, nor are heaven and hell even physical places—they are symbols, just like the term "God" is. And if God is a symbol for the Ground of Being, then heaven and hell can be seen as symbols for the level of spiritual development we have embodied during our life. The psychological and spiritual experience of feeling morally condemned (hell), or feeling morally fulfilled (heaven), highlights the degree to which we maintained our unity with God by cultivating love, meaning, healing, and purpose in our lives.

Even though he doesn't see heaven and hell as literal places, just like other religious symbols Tillich sees these as somewhat important because they point to basic psychological realities: 1) feeling that one has used one's life to become one's best self in existence, and thus felt connected to the Eternal (heaven), or 2) feeling that one has stayed under the power of existential estrangement and therefore not experienced the depth of life, or the Eternal (hell).

Unfortunately, the symbols of heaven and hell have been, and still are, often used inappropriately by religious authorities. They are used to instill fear (hell), or as a reward (heaven), to compel or entice a person into "proper" behavior. And both of these methods can lead to distorted and/or detrimental outcomes in the minds and lives of those who are under the spell of religious authorities who use these symbols as devices of control. Still, as symbols, Tillich believes that heaven and hell are apt expressions of inner psychological realities we face by virtue of our humanity and having to confront others and ourselves in the moral act:

> The frequently evil psychological effects of a literal use of 'heaven' and 'hell' are not sufficient reason for removing them completely. They provide vivid expression for the threat of 'death away from eternity,' and for its contrast, 'promise of eternal life.' One cannot 'psychologize away' basic experiences of threat and despair about the ultimate meaning of existence, as one cannot psychologize away

> moments of blessedness in anticipated fulfillment. Psychology can only dissolve the neurotic consequences of the literalistic distortion of the two symbols, and there is ample reason for it to do so.[157]

In these words Tillich emphasizes the heavy psychological weight of our moral actions, which could be seen on two extreme ends of the human spiritual experience; for example, 1) someone who is in the grips of an ecstatic feeling of the depth of life and senses the healing presence of the Eternal or, 2) someone who is in the grips of a crushing guilt from having wronged another person and feels alone, spiritually condemned, and estranged from the Eternal. The symbolism represented by heaven and hell reflects this seriousness. For Tillich, the significance of our actions extends beyond our death: the degree to which we become morally-centered and in touch with our essential self *in life* determines our participation *beyond life* in the Eternal.

Though Tillich's theory of essentialization highlights the seriousness of our moral decisions, what it does not allow for is the possibility of someone being eternally condemned. Most people struggle throughout life to actualize their essential self but, to varying degrees, succeed or fail. Sadly, many remain under the continual power of existential estrangement and its distorted morality, thus failing to experience the depth of life and the healing power of love. Others fall to the crippling power of consumerism and mass conformity, never even seeing beyond a synthetic, manufactured world that is incapable of offering anything other than fleeting moments of "happiness." And still some are subject to physical, biological, psychological, or sociological conditions preventing their adequate moral development. Tillich addresses this final issue when he speaks of distorted forms of life that are never able to reach their fulfillment even to the smallest degree: "premature destruction, the death of infants, biological and psychological disease, and Spiritually destructive environments."[158]

No matter which of these scenarios one may be in—and sometimes it's a combination of several of them—Tillich remains convinced of the universal participation of all beings in the Eternal Memory, or Eternal Life, of God. And this is the positive message of essentialization: even for those who have not largely succeeded in becoming their essential self, it "emphasizes the despair of having wasted one's potentialities yet also assures the elevation of the positive within existence (even in the most unfulfilled life) into eternity."[159] In other words, no one in existence can be seen as entirely good or entirely evil—the "sinner" participates in the "saint," and vice versa. In a rather long passage about humanity's *telos* (aim or goal), Tillich lays out his vision for what it means to actualize one's essential self and thus elevate one's participation in the Eternal after death:

> The symbol for this is Eternal Life, but it does not mean endless time or timelessness, as it is described in popular literature and religion. Man as finite freedom has a relation to Eternal Life which is different from that of

> beings under the predominance of necessity. Awareness of the element of 'ought to be,' and with it awareness of responsibility, guilt, despair, and hope, characterizes man's relation to the eternal. Everything temporal has a 'teleological' relation to the eternal, but man alone is aware of it; and this awareness gives him the freedom to turn against it. The Christian assertion of the tragic universality of estrangement implies that every human being turns against his *telos*, against Eternal Life, at the same time that he aspires to it. This makes the concept of 'essentialization' profoundly dialectical. The *telos* of man as an individual is determined by the decisions he makes in existence. . . He can waste his potentialities, though not completely, and he can fulfill them, though not totally. Thus, the symbol of ultimate judgment receives a particular seriousness. The exposure of the negative as negative may not leave much positive for Eternal Life. It can be a reduction to smallness; but it also can be an elevation to greatness.[160]

In the end, the moral imperative found in every human decision is what brings us face to face with our ultimate destiny; our moral actualization determines the depth and quality of our salvation, or healing—both in life and beyond life. But unlike all fundamentalist doctrines on salvation, Tillich sees every individual destiny as tied up with every other one. He emphasizes the idea that no one can be condemned to an eternal hell because we are all, in some sense, part of one destiny. He sums up his opposition to fundamentalist ideas on salvation, while laying out his own, by saying:

> From the point of view which assumes individual destinies, there is no answer at all. The question and the answer are possible only if one understands essentialization or elevation of the positive into Eternal Life as a matter of universal participation: in the essence of the least actualized individual, the essences of other individuals and, indirectly, of all beings are present. *Whoever condemns anyone to eternal death condemns himself, because his essence and that of the other cannot be absolutely separated.* And he who is estranged from his own essential being and experiences the despair of total self-rejection must be told that his essence participates in the essences of all those who have reached a high degree of fulfillment and that through his participation his being is eternally affirmed. (emphasis mine)[161]

In this vision of Tillich's is found the basis for the Christian concept of forgiveness. Throughout life, we struggle with the pains and challenges of human existence and, on some level, each one of us fails to become our fully essential self because of these struggles. In recognizing this—as well as in recognizing the fact that our individual destiny is tied up with every other human destiny—we understand that we need to forgive others just as much as we ourselves need forgiveness. Thus, when we condemn anyone else, we are also condemning ourselves.

In the end, the ultimate unity of life—including our unity with the natural world on the most microscopic of levels—prohibits us from thinking that we are somehow completely separated from the beings with whom we share our existence on earth: "What happens in time and space, in the smallest particle of matter as well as in the greatest personality, is significant for the eternal life."[162] If only humanity would come see the wisdom in these words and how they could humanize our existence.

ENDNOTES

Preface

1 Today, we often hear "I'm spiritual but not religious," or "I don't like 'organized' religion."
2 A modern materialist-religious doctrine—seen primarily in Christian evangelical fundamentalism—that sees financial wealth as a blessing from God.
3 Paul Tillich, *Systematic Theology* (University of Chicago Press: 1951, 1957, and 1963). Hereafter, referred to as ST 1, ST 2, or ST 3.
4 ST 2, 91.
5 ST 3, 184.
6 ST 3, 381.

Chapter 1

7 ST 1, 3.
8 ST 1, 277.
9 ST 1, 62.
10 Paul Tillich, "The Lost Dimension in Religion," *The Saturday Evening Post* 230, no. 50 (June 14, 1958).
11 James L. Jarrett, *Jung's Seminar on Nietzsche's Zarathustra* (Princeton, N.J., Princeton University Press, 1998), 124.
12 Paul Tillich, "The Lost Dimension in Religion," *The Saturday Evening Post* 230, no. 50 (June 14, 1958).
13 Paul Tillich, edited and introduced by J. Mark Thomas, *The Spiritual Situation in our Technical Society* (Georgia: Mercer University Press, 1988), 127.

14 ST 3, 62.
15 ST 3, 308.
16 Paul Tillich, edited and introduced by J. Mark Thomas, "The World Situation," in *The Spiritual Situation in our Technical Society* (Georgia: Mercer University Press, 1988), 6.
17 Ibid., p. 4.
18 Paul Tillich, "The Lost Dimension in Religion," *The Saturday Evening Post* 230, no. 50 (June 14, 1958).
19 ST 2, 41.
20 ST 2, 67.
21 ST 2, 29.
22 Ibid., p. 7.

Chapter 2
23 ST 3, 130.
24 William James, *The Varieties of Religious Experience* (New York: The Library of America, 1987), p. 116.
25 ST 2, 116-117.
26 ST 3, 227.
27 ST 1, 237.
28 Paul Tillich, *Theology of Culture* (New York: Oxford University, 1959), pp. 4-5.
29 ST 1, 238.
30 ST 1, 235. The philosophical term "categories of finitude," also known as the "categories of existence," is one used to describe the four basic ways we know and classify the world: *time* (a past, present, and future), *space* (a visible reality through which all things move), *causality* (one event

or object causing an effect on another), and *substance* (tangible, physical objects we see and touch).
31 ST 1, 211.
32 ST 1, 206.
33 ST 1, 205.
34 Projection is a term often used in psychology to describe the laying off of something inside one's own psyche onto someone, or something, else. For example, a cheating husband will "project" his guilt onto his wife by accusing her of cheating.
35 ST 1, 212.
36 Paul Tillich, *Biblical Religion and the Search for Ultimate Realty* (Chicago: University of Chicago, 1955), p. 13.
37 ST 1, 245.
38 Paul Tillich, "Science and Theology: A Discussion with Einstein," in *Theology of Culture* (New York: Oxford University Press, 1959), 130.
39 ST 1, 211.
40 Shunryu Suzuki, *Not Always So: Practicing the True Spirit of Zen* (HarperCollins Publishers, 2002), p. 56.

Chapter 3
41 Bart Ehrlich, *How Jesus Became God* (New York: HarperCollins, 2014), 73.
42 ST 1, 153.
43 ST 3, 19.
44 Paul Tillich, edited and introduced by J. Mark Thomas, "Expressions of Man's Self-Understanding in Philosophy

and the Sciences," in *The Spiritual Situation in our Technical Society* (Georgia: Mercer University Press, 1988), 100.
45 William James, *The Varieties of Religious Experience* (New York: The Library of America, 1987), p. 159.
46 ST 1, 149.

Chapter 4
47 ST 1, 110.
48 ST 1, 117.
49 ST 1, 133.
50 ST 1, 115.
51 ST 2, 161.
52 ST 2, 155.
53 ST 2, 155.
54 ST 2, 156.
55 ST 2, 156.
56 ST 2, 157.
57 ST 2, 157.
58 ST 1, 49.
59 Paul Tillich, *The New Being* (New York: Charles Scribner's Sons, 1955), 24.
60 ST 1, 111-112.
61 Jeremy D. Yunt, *Faithful to Nature: Paul Tillich and the Spiritual Roots of Environmental Ethics* (Barred Owl Books, 2017).
62 ST 1, 121.

Chapter 5
63 Paul Tillich, *Christianity and the Encounter of World Religions* (Minneapolis: Fortress Press, 1994), 62.

64   ST 2, 44.
65   ST 2, 45.
66   Paul Tillich, edited and introduced by J. Mark Thomas, "The World Situation," in *The Spiritual Situation in our Technical Society* (Georgia: Mercer University Press, 1988), 20-21.
67   ST 3, 388.
68   ST 2, 26.
69   ST 3, 107.
70   ST 3, 206.
71   ST 3, 207.
72   ST 3, 245.
73   ST 2, 134.
74   ST 2, 12.
75   ST 3, 275.
76   ST 3, 245.
77   ST 3, 112.
78   ST 3, 231.
79   ST 3, 231-232.
80   ST 3, 232.
81   ST 3, 233.
82   ST 3, 234.
83   ST 3, 235.
84   ST 3, 235-236.
85   ST 3, 235.
86   ST 3, 131.
87   ST 3, 153.
88   ST 3, 207.
89   ST 3, 243.

90   ST 3, 151-152.
91   ST 3, 134.
92   ST 3, 136.
93   ST 1, 280.
94   ST 1, 280.
95   ST 1, 279.

Chapter 6
96   ST 2, 46-47.
97   ST 2, 49.
98   ST 2, 46.
99   ST 2, 47.
100 ST 2, 49.
101 ST 2, 49.
102 ST 2, 50-51.
103 ST 2, 52.
104 ST 2, 61.
105 ST 2, 60.
106 ST 2, 47.

Chapter 7
107 ST 3, 5.
108 ST 3, 16.
109 ST 3, 20.
110 ST 3, 17.
111 ST 3, 26.
112 ST 3, 21.
113 ST 3, 21.
114 ST 3, 26.

115 ST 1, 260.
116 ST 3, 19.
117 Jeremy D. Yunt, *Faithful to Nature: Paul Tillich and the Spiritual Roots of Environmental Ethics* (Barred Owl Books, 2017).
118 ST 1, 261.

Chapter 8
119 ST 2, 97.
120 ST 2, 97-98.
121 ST 1, 133.
122 ST 1, 148.
123 ST 2, 93.
124 ST 2, 94.
125 ST 2, 126.
126 ST 2, 133.
127 ST 1, 135.
128 ST 2, 131.
129 ST 1, 133.
130 ST 3, 243.
131 ST 2, 27.
132 ST 2, 161.
133 ST 2, 88.
134 ST 2, 92.
135 ST 2, 102.
136 ST 2, 148.
137 ST 2, 116.
138 ST 2, 114.
139 ST 3, 223.

Chapter 9

140 ST 1, 152.
141 ST 2, 166.
142 ST 2, 147.
143 Paul Tillich, *The Meaning of Health: Essays in Existentialism, Psychoanalysis, and Religion* (Chicago: Exploration Press, 1984), 16.
144 ST 3, 408.
145 ST 3, 407.
146 Paul Tillich, *The Shaking of the Foundations* (New York: C. Scribner's Sons Press, 1955), 84.
147 ST 2, 96.
148 This is why we see in the Bible the vision of the lion lying down with the lamb. Interestingly, today we see species that would normally eat a prey, instead taking care of it. The most recent example I've seen is a leopard killing an adult baboon, and then instinctively protecting its prey orphaned baby baboon from hyenas. Science is still trying to determine the motivations for this behavior, but it certainly has important moral implications for the entire world if it's proven that moral concern can evolve in a trans-species way.
149 Paul Tillich, "Man and Earth," in *The Eternal Now* (New York: Charles Scribner's Sons, 1963), 74.
150 ST 2, 167.
151 Paul Tillich, "The Eternal Now," in *The Eternal Now* (New York: Charles Scribner's Sons, 1963), 131.
152 ST 3, 400.

Chapter 10
153 ST 1, 270.
154 Paul Tillich, "The Eternal Now," in *The Eternal Now* (New York: Charles Scribner's Sons, 1963), 125.
155 ST 3, 417.
156 ST 3, 401.
157 ST 3, 419.
158 ST 3, 409.
159 ST 3, 407.
160 ST 3, 406.
161 ST 3, 409.
162 ST 3, 397-398.

ABOUT THE AUTHOR

Jeremy D. Yunt is an independent scholar with a Master's degree in Ethics (Philosophy) and Depth Psychology from the GTU, Berkeley, CA. A long-time member of the North American Paul Tillich Society, he has published four books, as well as articles in *Philosophy Now* (UK), the *Journal of Humanistic Psychology*, and the *Journal of Animal Ethics*.

Printed in Great Britain
by Amazon